PUBLIC POLICYMAKING

by

PRIVATE ORGANIZATIONS

PUBLIC POLICYMAKING

by

PRIVATE ORGANIZATIONS

Challenges to Democratic Governance

CATHERINE E. RUDDER
A. LEE FRITSCHLER
YON JUNG CHOI

BROOKINGS INSTITUTION PRESS

Washington, D.C.

The Brookings Institution is a private nonprofit organization devoted
to research, education, and publication on important issues of domestic and foreign policy. Its principal purpose is to bring the highest
quality independent research and analysis to bear on current and
emerging policy problems. Interpretations or conclusions in Brookings
publications should be understood to be solely those of the authors.

Library of Congress Cataloging-in-Publication data are on file.

ISBN 978-0-8157-2898-6 (pbk)
ISBN 978-0-8157-2899-3 (ebook)

9 8 7 6 5 4 3 2 1

Typeset in Simoncini Garamond

Composition by Westchester Publishing Services

To Richard Hofstetter

Whose life, wisdom, and instruction
have inspired this work

Everyone has experienced how learning an appropriate name for what was dim and vague cleared up and crystallized the whole matter.

John Dewey

To alter concepts . . . is to alter behavior.

Alasdair MacIntyre

CONTENTS

INTRODUCTION

With this book we make the case that private governance—binding rules made by nongovernmental groups that affect the opportunities and welfare of the broader public—is a significant and growing phenomenon. It should be recognized by professionals and studied and investigated as a distinct field of inquiry by policy scholars. We also believe that journalists should report on private governing activities as systematically as other beats and that those activities should be opened to public scrutiny.

An earlier book written by two of us, *Smoking and Politics: Bureaucracy Centered Policymaking*,[1] focuses on legislatures' delegation of decisionmaking authority to permit rulemaking by government agencies. This new volume expands the policymaking spectrum to include the policymaking work of private organizations. Taken together, agency rulemaking and the policy decisions of private groups account for most policymaking in advanced societies.[2] Yet this key point is largely ignored by those who study, teach, and report on public policy issues today. Most curricula in public policy and political science contain few or no references to policymaking outside the realms of legislatures, elected chief executives, and courts. Most newspapers and other non-specialized media pay too little detailed attention to agency rulemaking and almost none to the setting of authoritative regulations, rules, and standards by private groups.

Since the mid-2000s, the three of us have been working on aspects of the topic of private governance. Catherine E. Rudder has published in the area, identifying and illustrating its myriad workings and wrestling with the difficulties that this domain poses.[3] A. Lee Fritschler has been involved in higher education issues as a college president and assistant secretary in the U.S. Department of Education and has published a number of short pieces related to the subject of this book. And Yon Jung Choi has been a student of the subject in our classes and others. Her ideas and views from the perspective of student and Ph.D. candidate have added an important dimension to this work, as has her research on corporate social responsibility.[4]

Perhaps the most problematic aspect of the concept of private governance is the distinction between the words *public* and *private*, in that the division does not hold once private governance is exposed. This book shows that private governance is actually public, both that which is delegated by statute to a private group and that which arises independently.[5] If private governance is not considered public, the idea that people in democratic societies live in communities largely of their own collective making loses meaning. By accepting private governance as private, people lose control over much of what shapes their lives, their opportunities, health, and welfare. At the same time, to interfere with private governance is to risk losing some of its contributions to providing the high-level expertise needed for intelligent policymaking today, responsiveness to technological change, networks that reduce the global governance gap, and alternatives to the state.

Another difficulty that the concept of private governance poses is that few people have ever heard of it, much less can define it. In fact, defining it so that it can be identified and studied systematically is, we think, a major achievement of this book. We will also welcome the sharpening and honing of the ideas presented here. That is one of the purposes of this work.

We make the point that private governance is not the same as privatization, as the uninitiated tend to assume. It is not in the realm of lobbying, another common misperception. Nor should private governance be called "self-governance" or "self-regulation" or "market-based regulation."[6] To do so is to obscure the public impact of private rules and to deny the claims of outsiders to be formally represented. When supposed self-governance creates significant impact beyond a group's members, self-governance becomes governance of others and should be recognized as such. When self-governance is used as an alternative to government, it simply substitutes private decisionmakers for democratically legitimate ones.

Many of the organizations engaged in private governance do not confine their activities to determining rules and making policy that others must follow. Anyone studying private governance organizations needs to recognize this fact. These groups may also publish professional journals, hold conferences, sell products and services, promote their industry through lobbying and political contributions, or engage in work with little or no relevance to our topic.

Adding further to the confusion about private governance is that no single type of organization engages in such policymaking. Private governance groups include multinational, for-profit corporations as well as not-for-profit organizations of various sorts, and therefore can be difficult to identify. We make the point that without a clear definition of private governance, citizens and scholars will not be able to recognize who these groups are and what they are doing. Questions about their legitimacy in a democratic society cannot be raised if people are not able to spot private governance in the first place. As the writer Robertson Davies in the novel *Tempest-Tost* reminds his readers, "The eye sees only what the mind is prepared to comprehend."[7]

An important obstruction in recognizing private governance is the fact that much of it is intertwined with governments. The federal government, for example, *mandates* membership in some of these groups and the payment of fees to them. Sometimes it *creates* a private organization and gives it policymaking and enforcement responsibilities. Often it delegates its powers to private entities, and it *enforces* rules made by independent groups, as this volume demonstrates. State and local governments adopt into law building codes developed by private groups.[8] The professions are largely governed by their own bodies, and governments at all levels rely on their choices.

Beyond defining private governance and identifying in chapters 1 and 2 where and why it exists, we have sought in subsequent chapters to pinpoint its importance in democratic society and illustrate how it works in some detail. We have chosen three broad areas—finance, food safety, and the professions—and have dug into some of the private organizations making policy in these fields. We want to make concrete what might otherwise seem to be a nebulous concept. The areas we have chosen are quite different from one another, demonstrating the breadth and considerable variety of the workings of private governance and reflecting the authors' interests. We want to highlight the scope of private policymaking and demonstrate that it affects nearly everyone, nearly all the time, in quite disparate areas of policy.

Chapter 3 first focuses on how to assess private governance. To the degree that private groups are making public choices about values to pursue, they should be evaluated on the grounds of democratic legitimacy, including the organizations' inclusiveness, transparency, and accountability in their governance roles, just as government should be.

A significant deficiency of private governance is its lack of accountability and, specifically, the fact that it is riddled with potential conflicts of interest. The decisions of conflicted groups are likely to serve the groups themselves and much less likely to serve the public, if the interests of the two are not congruent. The epistemic biases of experts and professionals working within their own organizations lean toward the fields to which they have given their lives. Old saws like "Who would know better than your mother?" or "The fox is guarding the hen house" spring to mind. As we detail specific examples in chapters 4 through 6, we look for the degree to which each group adheres to public-regarding and democratic precepts rhetorically and actually. We try to describe exactly how private rulemaking works for good or ill, as well as make some suggestions for improvement.

Although we wholeheartedly agree with Giandomenico Majone that completely separating technical decisions from value choices in public policymaking is next to impossible, we argue that the more technical a group's decisions, the more the public needs to rely on them, presuming that the technical decisions are undergirded by values the public would endorse.[9] The public has no capacity to determine physical layer specifications in information technology, but the public surely desires that information technology work as seamlessly as possible.[10]

Our acceptance of Majone's idea that technical and value decisions are difficult to disentangle requires another bow to this policy scholar. Specifically, we embrace his idea that democratic society needs more translators between science and the public—that is, professionals who understand highly technical matters in a particular area, who can identify the value choices entailed in selecting, for example, one technology over another, who can create meaningful categories to facilitate public debate, and who can help mediate between scientists and public policymakers. With the exponential increase in scientific knowledge, such translators or policy professionals are needed now more than ever. If democracy should be conceived as government by discussion, as the philosopher John Dewey argued, then that conversation needs to be facilitated by such translators.[11]

Because of the advantages of private governance, including expertise and speed, and, in comparison, the seeming dysfunction of American democracy today, a common reaction to this volume might be, "Thank goodness for private governance! What a mess the country and the world would be in without it."[12] Perhaps this response makes sense for the present, but if people together want to make choices for themselves and control their destinies to a larger degree, they must not give up on democratic government or on having a say in the policies that impinge significantly on their lives. At the least they should demand that private governance be subject to scrutiny and to democratic standards. If private governance is here to stay and continues to grow, as we argue, then the groups that make rules for the rest of society must not be permitted to operate with impunity, that is, with little transparency and public oversight.

New theorizing about democratic arrangements will be needed to accommodate private governance, to make it as accountable, transparent, and inclusive as possible. If the public is to be represented, more theorizing is needed to determine how to create a scheme of representation outside of the current governmental forms.[13] Citizens cannot do their job of securing a democratic society until scholars do theirs by recognizing private governance, suggesting mechanisms for a public role in making value choices, and systematically studying and teaching about this field of inquiry as an overarching whole.

Readers interested in finding precursors, in a sense, to this volume would do well to consult Grant McConnell's *Private Power and American Democracy* (New York: Random House, 1966), Harold Lasswell's *Politics: Who Gets What, When and How?* (New York: McGraw-Hill, 1936), Theodore Lowi's *The End of Liberalism: The Second Republic of the United States* (New York: W. W. Norton, 1979, rev. 2009), and Susan Strange's *The Retreat of the State: The Diffusion of Power in the World Economy* (Cambridge University Press, 1996).

Our intention is that this volume will be helpful to advanced undergraduate and graduate students studying public policy, academic colleagues in public policy, reporters, private standard-setters, government officials, and the attentive public. Courses in disciplines outside of public policy, public administration, and political science—for example, journalism, business, law, sociology, finance, and public management, and specific policy areas such as health, food safety, agriculture, and higher education—would also benefit from considering the ideas presented here.

The authors wish to thank our colleagues James Garand, Kay Schlozman, and Sue Tolleson Rinehart, who provided useful feedback and encouragement in the early stages of this project; our former students Michelle Ranville, Paul Weissburg, Phillip Magness, Snigda Dewall, and Eun Jung Park for their assistance and good ideas; freelance editor extraordinaire Alison Howard, who worked with us throughout the project and made this book more accessible to a wider audience; our friends Catherine Pagano, Joyce Murdoch, and John Gist, who read and critiqued all or part of the manuscript; our partners Susan T. Fritschler, Helen Gibson, and Timothy Koncewicz for their patience and encouragement; Rachel Feinstein, who contributed an account of her organization's experience with private governance; our many students and colleagues at George Mason, who have added much to our thinking on this topic; the editors at the Brookings Institution Press, including William Finan, Robert Faherty, and Janet Walker for their support; and copyeditor Janet Mowery.

One

WHAT IS PRIVATE GOVERNANCE?

When the U.S. real estate bubble burst in 2007 and precipitated a global financial crisis, among the least visible perpetrators were the top three credit-rating agencies, which gave the highest, safest ratings to mortgages that were bundled into extremely risky securities and sold to investors. Credit raters are paid by the companies that issue securities, and those companies shop among the agencies for the best rating. The resulting conflict of interest produced ratings that ill-served the public and investors alike while it enriched those who created, misrated, and sold the garbage investment vehicles.

When city of Detroit employees were forced in 2014 to accept severe cuts in their pension payouts to avert the total collapse of their retirement fund, some of the blame should have fallen to the Governmental Accounting Standards Board (GASB), which creates the regulations followed by states and localities for financial statements and was slow to make rules to help ensure that pensions and retiree benefits are adequately funded.

Students purchase a microwave oven for their dorm room. They plug it into an electrical outlet anywhere in the United States and it operates perfectly without smoke, fire, or electrical shock. Standards for the sockets and safeguards for the oven are in place thanks to the work of companies such as UL (formerly Underwriters Laboratories), which certifies that products are safe.

What do credit-rating agencies, the GASB, and UL in the examples above have in common? They are "private governance" institutions: private groups whose decisions become public policy, dramatically affecting people's lives with little or no public participation or scrutiny. At the same time, they serve important public purposes that governmental bodies may be ill-suited to address. These groups are found everywhere—in finance, commerce, industry, and the professions. Among many other public functions, these organizations certify professionals and tradespeople as competent, establish industry regulations, and set technical and professional standards that give them broad reach into people's lives and have an enormous impact on society.

But because their operations lack the transparency and accountability required of governmental bodies, these groups constitute a policymaking territory that is largely unseen, unreported outside of trade publications, uncharted, and not easily reconciled with democratic principles. As such, that territory demands to be fully explored, documented, and understood. To put the matter even more urgently, private governance should be recognized—and scrutinized—as a distinct and important area in the field of public policy.

PUBLIC POLICY, PRIVATELY MADE

Societies are governed by rules, some of them informal but widely acknowledged such as social norms and professional expectations and some codified as laws and regulations. Most people learn that laws and regulations are enacted by public governmental bodies that, in democracies, derive their authority from a constitutional right to rule and to have their decisions enforced by the courts via governmental intermediaries—for example, the police, the U.S. Department of Justice, and the U.S. Securities and Exchange Commission (SEC). In a democratic society, government institutions operate according to principles that require transparency, public participation, equal justice, and the rule of law, and they maintain publicly available records of their actions and decisions.[1] This boilerplate description of the elements of public policymaking and enforcement is woefully incomplete, however, in that it omits a significant area of formal governance not subject to democratic principles and representative government.

Specifically, private groups also make and enforce rules that function like governments' laws and regulations.

Distinguishing five arenas of policymaking in the United States can help explain why private governance institutions must be included in any map of the American public policy universe. Three of these arenas—legislatures, which enact laws; the executive branch with its administrative agencies, which make and enforce rules to implement the laws; and the judiciary, which enforces and also makes policy through its decisions—are generally well understood. Unfortunately, in much of the political science and policy literature, they are depicted as the entire policy world. They are covered thoroughly in academic literature and discussed widely among the interested or attentive public.

A fourth arena is not as well understood by the public and receives much less academic attention than the first three. This fourth arena consists of hybrid agencies that are created by government but operate with varying degrees of independence from government and its resources and often take on organizational forms unlike those of regular government agencies.

For example, the Federal Reserve, the central bank of the United States, contains some private elements but is a very powerful governmental policymaker that has been intentionally distanced from representative government.[2] The seven-member Federal Reserve Board of Governors, the heart of the system, is today the most significant financial regulator in the country and perhaps in the world, and the Federal Reserve's Federal Open Market Committee is a powerful monetary policymaking body. Other examples of fourth-arena institutions created by the federal government are the Pension Benefit Guarantee Corporation, the Tennessee Valley Authority, Amtrak, and the Federal National Mortgage Association (Fannie Mae), to name only a few.[3] States, too, have their own hybrids in such forms as special authorities and interstate compacts. Some hybrid institutions are significant policymakers, while others are not.[4]

Least well understood by the public or policy analysts is a largely unseen fifth arena: *private* organizations that make *public* policy. These are the primary focus of this book, along with the policymaking parts of the fourth arena. It is unseen because it is not typically recognized as a distinct arena of public policymaking at all. Some private organizations shape the distribution of resources in society and govern behavior in a fashion similar to that of governmental bodies, with an important exception: the rules under which they operate do not require transparency, equal justice, clearly defined public participation, freely available statements of the standards they set, or other democratic strictures. They are not systematically accountable to a representative assembly of the public, and are even less so to the public directly. Nonetheless, the decisions of private groups in the fifth arena are enforceable by various means and often by government itself, including courts and federal agencies. A very large number and assortment of these private organizations make policies that affect the larger public—their health and safety, their quality of life, and the opportunities and choices available to them. But these private entities' authoritative rulemaking functions are often concealed by the variety of forms they take; they include trade associations, professional societies, and not-for-profit organizations. In fact, even a for-profit enterprise may include private governance as one of its activities.

The federal government has stimulated the development, growth, and authority of private groups and defers to their decisions. In 1996, for example, Congress passed the National Technology Transfer and Advancement Act (NTTAA), which expanded the reach of the fifth arena. The act states, in part, that "all federal agencies and departments shall use standards that are developed or adopted by voluntary consensus standards bodies, using such technical standards as a means to carry out policy objectives."[5] The word used is *shall*, not *may,* and it requires executive branch agencies to rely on the rulemaking of private bodies. Although the law makes exceptions to this instruction, its main effect is to empower private rulemaking and to tie the work of private organizations to that of government agencies. Not only does the law convey substantial power to private groups, but it seems to have widened the policymaking activities of private organizations in recent years.

Groups that fall into the fifth arena of policymaking can be difficult to identify. The variety in their organizational types is considerable and their policy work can range from accreditation to certification to standard-setting and regulation, and sometimes enforcement. Another obstacle to recognizing such groups is that their purpose is often much broader than—and often unrelated to—making rules and setting and enforcing standards. For instance, a fifth-arena private governance group might also perform the regular tasks of an industry trade group, such as lobbying governments and holding conferences, but such activities are not part of private governance as we define it in this book. Further, private groups, as self-governing organizations, design regulations for their own operations in the form of bylaws and other wholly internal rules, and those types of self-governance are also not addressed here.[6] Hence, it can be difficult to distinguish between a private group, like a trade association or club, and a private governance group that is also a trade association. Private governance groups do not declare themselves as such, and ordinary language does not direct observers to the existence of such groups.

To summarize, private governance is the public policymaking work of some fourth- and all fifth-arena institutions. Though widespread, private governance and the institutions that engage in it can be difficult to recognize and can be connected to government to one degree or another. In turn, formal public scrutiny of the work of these groups also varies.

HOW TO IDENTIFY A PRIVATE GOVERNANCE GROUP

It is clear that private governance groups take different organizational forms and engage in a variety of policymaking activities. But how exactly is one to identify an organization that is engaged in private governance? To do so, one must pinpoint the specific activity of rulemaking, its acceptance, and its impact—in other words, one must define private governance. As noted, it comprises decisions and standards that are made by private groups but function, in effect, as public policy. Specifically, such decisions and standards are characterized by three elements: They are *authoritative*, they affect a *broader public* beyond the group's members, and they have a *substantial impact*.

Rules made by private groups become "authoritative" in one or more of the following ways: first, tacit acceptance of their decisions by the public, as in the case of safety standards set by UL or professional licensing organizations; second, explicit reference to the rules and their acceptance as determinative in court, as in the judiciary's use of privately crafted safety standards to identify industry best practices and to determine the outcome of cases; third, enforcement of privately made rules by a governmental agency, as when the SEC enforces privately created accounting standards; fourth, tacit or explicit legal recognition of the group and its determinations, which is one source of the power of Standard & Poor's and other credit-rating companies; fifth, legal command, as in the case of the NTTAA, discussed above; and last, their incorporation by local, state, or federal government into law, as in the case of privately developed higher education accreditation standards or those of the American Bar Association (ABA). Other examples of authoritative standard-setters include the American Correctional Association, the International Code Council (ICC), the Association of American Railroads, the American Petroleum Institute, the National Association of Home Builders (NAHB), and the American Society of Heating and Air-Conditioning Engineers (ASHRAE).

The phrase "affecting a broader public" indicates that the rules apply to or touch many more people than those who make them and the sectors they represent. For example, oil and gas pipeline safety standards that are privately made concern not only the rulemakers and their industry but also other industries throughout the supply chain, residents near the pipeline, and the environment. Similarly, safety standards for harnesses used to hoist workers at construction sites not only apply to the contractors but also affect the workers who rely on the standards to protect them and the general public, which pays for the cost of compliance in higher construction costs and rents. Another example is the certification of surgeons: state governments use standards set by private medical associations to determine who can operate on patients; those standards affect not only the professional lives of doctors but also the safety of everyone who undergoes surgery. Similarly, state, local, and federal governments variously mandate Leadership in Energy and Environmental Design (LEED) standards created by the private U.S. Green Building Council. LEED standards, in turn, require use of specific private standards created by other nongovernmental groups.[7]

Private governance rules have a "substantial impact" in that they exert influence across sectors, industries, and territories. Private food safety standards, for example, affect other sectors and industries such as delivery and packaging, the food service industry, U.S. governmental agencies (such as the Food and Drug Administration, the Department of Agriculture's Food Safety and Inspection Service, and the Environmental Protection Agency), labor unions, and consumer groups, and, at times, food regulations of foreign countries, not to mention the health of the public. One reasonable test of "substantial impact" is to ask whether contemporary society could do without the rules made by private groups. That is, if a private group had not made the rule or set the standard, would government need to make it or set it in the interest of the health, safety, or welfare of the public? At the same time, however, to be *substantially affected,* a broader public need not be aware of the content of specific rules, such as electrical standards, building codes, or credit ratings for corporations and governments.

HOW PREVALENT IS PRIVATE GOVERNANCE?

Because the fifth arena has not been recognized as a significant area of policymaking, no data have been collected on it as a whole. Nevertheless, assembling the fragmentary evidence that does exist provides

TABLE 1-1. *Estimated Number of Standards*
in the United States, 1967–2014

Sector	1967	1984	1991	1996	Current (2014)
Government	39,500	49,000	52,500	44,000	Fewer than 50,000
Private	14,000	32,000	41,500	49,000	More than 50,000
Total	53,500	81,000	94,000	93,000	More than 100,000

Sources: The figures are from several sources: John E. Hartman, *Directory of United States Standardization Activities* (Washington, D.C.: NBS, Department of Commerce, 1967); Robert B. Toth, *Standards Activities of Organizations in the United States* (Washington, D.C.: NIST Special Publication 806, U.S. Department of Commerce, 1996); and ANSI website, at www.ansi .org/about_ansi/introduction/introduction.aspx?menuid=1.

glimpses into its pervasiveness. The most recognizable form of private governance is standard-setting, and the scope and number of fifth-arena standards in place is surprising. Considering that most discussions of U.S. policymaking ignore private governance, it should also be alarming.

Unfortunately, the most current available data on U.S. standards are found in the 1996 "Standards Activities of Organizations" published by the Department of Commerce's National Institute of Standards and Technology (NIST). Projecting from this data source, the American National Standards Institute, a private governance group, has estimated that there are more than 100,000 standards in the country today, more than half of them created by the private sector (see table 1-1). However, these figures likely are underestimated since these mostly technical standards are at least twenty years old and do not include state- and local-level standards and activities that "develop . . . ethical/professional standards, or that set standards for judging ani-

FIGURE 1-1. *Number of Private Standards Substituted for Public Standards, 1998–2011*

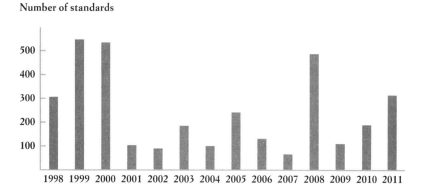

Number of standards

Sources: Fifteenth Annual Report on Federal Agency Use of Voluntary Consensus Standards and Conformity Assessment (Washington, D.C.: National Institute of Standards and Technology, Department of Commerce, 2012).

mals."[8] Because the excluded standards cover, for example, those set by the American Medical Association (AMA) and the Chartered Financial Analysts Institute (a global association of investment professionals), the actual number of both governmental and private standards is far greater than the published estimates.

As of 1996 nearly 700 U.S. organizations had produced and maintained standards, and an overwhelming majority of these organizations were nongovernmental agencies (604 were nongovernmental and 80 were governmental organizations).[9] Since the passage of the NTTAA, the substitution of private standards for public standards has continued steadily, if unevenly, as illustrated in figure 1-1.

From 1998 (when NIST first began to report on the effect of the 1996 act) to 2011, a total of 3,579 public standards were replaced by private standards. Federal agencies that have adopted private standards include the U.S. Departments of Defense, Commerce, and Health and Human Services. Despite the patchy nature of available data, these reports constitute the best, if greatly underestimated and

BOX 1-1. *Example of the Multiple Sources of Private Rules One Industry Must Follow*

From Rachel Feinstein, government affairs manager of the Hearth, Patio and Barbecue Association, for distribution on September 12, 2014.

Members of the Hearth, Patio and Barbecue Association are affected most by the private International Code Council's International Energy Conservation Codes (IECC) (see http://reca-codes.org/about-iecc.php).

These codes are updated every three years and cost about $44 per code, for people who are not members of the ICC, to purchase.

One controversial update recently made by the ICC is that voting on code changes has been moved from in-person voting to being able to vote online. Members of the public can attend code hearings and submit public comments, but this new online voting system makes the final voting process less transparent.

One thing we deal with is the states adopt the ICC codes, but they can make changes to them, which means this international code is further edited at the state level making it difficult to keep track of. I'm working on developing what we call a State Code Coordinator Program for our members. We would have 2 of our members in each state, familiar with codes and standards, keep track of the code adoption process as well as licensing issues and state legislation and regulations. It is very, very difficult to keep track of everything.

The private National Fire Protection Association (NFPA) also creates codes for builders. Voting members of NFPA are generally builders and installers, but recently, there have been more members with inspector and safety backgrounds. This has made some of the codes unrealistic and likely not what consumers want. For example, the NFPA 211 Committee on Chimneys, Fireplaces, Vents, and Solid Fuel-Burning Appliances recently proposed that only items that have been tested and listed for use in a specific model fireplace system may be used, both in the original installations and in replacements. This means that if a consumer wanted to change the grate in their fireplace, or change the mantel, an installer would not be able to do this because of the code. The proposal comes from fire safety concerns (accessories/parts not originally tested with a fireplace could cause a fire because it hasn't been tested with the unit). This proposal is available for public comment, but anyone outside of the industry may find it difficult to navigate the page or even know that this issue even exists.

The following private organizations also develop codes and standards that are applicable to our industry:

National Association of Home Builders (NAHB)

American Society of Heating and Air-Conditioning Engineers (ASHRAE)

Canadian Standards Association (CSA) makes codes that are used in the U.S. too

ASTM International

American Gas Association (AGA)

National Fuel Gas Code of the National Fire Protection Association (NFPA)

UL (formerly Underwriters Laboratories)

hard-to-capture, information on the prevalence of private governance. Internationally, private rulemaking is common but not systematically documented. A partial exception to this dearth of data is provided by Tim Büthe and Walter Mattli in their path-breaking book *The New Global Rulers*, which documents widespread private global governance in financial services.[10]

Taken together, these data strongly suggest that the amount of private standard-setting exceeds that of government in many areas, both in the United States and globally. Yet many policy scholars and the public seem unaware of the existence, much less the consequences, of private regulation. An example of the extensiveness of private governance as applied to a single, relatively small industry is recounted by Rachel Feinstein of the Hearth, Patio and Barbecue Association (see box 1-1).

WHY DOES PRIVATE GOVERNANCE GO LARGELY UNRECOGNIZED?

Despite its importance and rapid growth, private governance is hiding in plain sight, camouflaged by more familiar categories and the absence of its own recognized niche. What makes private governance difficult to identify is, first, that it is infrequently covered in studies of public policy, with many notable exceptions in the business literature and the international arena.[11] More often, practitioners are likely to know of the groups operating in their areas of expertise. Accountants are keenly aware of the Financial Accounting Standards Board (FASB), engineers of the Institute of Electrical and Electronics Engineers (IEEE), builders of the International Code Council, and so on.

Second, because these groups make decisions largely in private, information about these processes is not readily available in many cases, and, as a consequence, few researchers are able to consider their public impact. Private governance is protected, in the case of commercial enterprises, by the legal right to hold close proprietary data, and, in the case of nonprofit organizations, by the constitutional right to privacy. Often standards are sold by the group creating them, a practice that greatly restricts their availability.

Third, much of private governance, like standard-setting, is seen as "technical," requiring the direct participation, and even control, of experts who hold commercial or professional rather than governmental positions. It is commonly asserted that if enterprises to which rules apply control the development of those rules, the rules are more likely to be followed and less likely to be circumvented or gamed. Also, it is plausible to believe that most people feel expertise-based rulemaking is beyond their purview and should be left to private actors.

Fourth, private governance in the United States in particular has developed historically in tandem with increased government regulation. In many ways, private governance may seem like "the way we've always done it" and thus goes largely unnoticed. Coupled with the respect that private enterprise enjoys in this country, it probably comes as no surprise and causes no concern that, for example, the American National Standards Institute (ANSI), a private organization, represents the United States at the International Organization for Standardization (ISO).

Fifth, although we contend in this book that fifth-arena private governance should not be confused with the fourth arena, hybrid governance, sometimes the difference between the two can be minimal. For example, governments may encourage the use of private standards by public agencies, as in the case of the 1996 NTTAA and Circular A-119 published by the Office of Management and Budget (OMB).[12] They may adopt as law privately developed rules, as in the case of building codes, construction safety standards, licensing requirements to practice crafts, and prerequisites to practice law and medicine. Governments also may enforce privately made standards, as the SEC docs in imposing the accounting provisions established by the FASB on publicly traded companies. State and local governments may agree to be governed by the rules established by the private Governmental Accounting Standards Board, as most state and local governments are.

Hence, when some states legislate that their Supreme Courts determine who can practice law within their territories, casual observers may think that states, via their courts, control licensing of their lawyers, but underneath this technical direction lies the hegemony of the legal profession itself. In thirty-three states, practicing lawyers must belong to the state bar association, which decides who may practice law in the state.[13] In other states, such as New York, state boards composed of lawyers decide what credentials an individual must have to practice law, such as graduating from an institution accredited by the American Bar Association and passing the state bar exam, a test created by the state bar association and the ABA. In such cases, governments push decisions to private bodies.

In other areas, such as higher education accreditation, the federal government is seizing control of a process that has been privately run since its inception. When a government expropriates for its own purposes a private regulatory process, the private group can lose its independence. At the same time, to the degree that its decisions take on the force of law, the private organization can gain in stature, size, and financial wherewithal. A leading example of this consequence is the reliance the federal government has placed on a commission (the Joint Commission on Accreditation of Health Care Organizations) to determine which health facilities, such as hospitals, are eligible for Medicaid and Medicare funds, without which most of these institutions would be unable to stay afloat financially.[14]

In short, government may use private groups to make its public decisions. Sometimes the groups serve their own professional interests; sometimes the groups are co-opted by government for its purposes and lose some of their independence. Why does that matter? In a democracy, a process with the imprimatur of constitutional government should not be privately controlled. Further, according to the principle of limited government, public entities should not take over the work of private groups and in so doing subvert pluralistic society. Here lies a critical issue in private governance: when is it simply a part of a pluralistic society, limiting the reach of ever-expanding governments, and when does it undermine citizens' ability to control significant collective decisions in which they have every right to participate?

In sum, private governance comes in so many incarnations that identifying its existence is particularly difficult and perhaps impossible for those who are not already on the alert for it. Before the phenomenon can be identified, the concept of private governance needs to exist in the first place. As Ludwig Wittgenstein famously observed, "The limits of my language mean the limits of my world."[15] However, the concept of private governance is slippery. It does not always operate exclusively of governments. Governments are deeply implicated in private governance, and indeed their agents may participate in it, as staff members of the Environmental Protection Agency do in serving as "public representatives" on private standard-setting bodies.

WHY IS PRIVATE GOVERNANCE IMPORTANT?

With the rapid pace of technological innovation and economic globalization and the concomitant need for common standards and supply-chain consistency across borders, private governance, already widespread, is growing rapidly, filling governmental gaps. Yet the public has little way of knowing about it, much less influencing its decisions. Even though accrediting groups such as ANSI require that standards created under its aegis follow some of the procedures to which government agencies must adhere, such conditions clearly are not a substitute for representative democracy; nor do they have the same effect in private settings that they do in governmental ones.[16] Other groups do not even try to emulate the care ANSI imposes. In any case, operating largely in the shadows to create and sell proprietary standards excludes the public.[17] Rather than "of, by, and for the people," private governance could be described as of, by, and for commercial and privileged interests in the first instance with public interests as a subordinate consideration.[18]

Despite scattered efforts to reserve a place at the decisionmaking table for the "public," little careful analysis has been undertaken to understand conceptually or operationally who this public is or how officially designated "public representatives" in private groups see and perform their tasks. Most often, the public representative is a surrogate in the form of an official from a labor union or nonprofit organization (such as an environmental group), an academic expert, or a staff representative of a government agency—a far cry from the kind of representation found in legislatures or indirect representation (one step removed from, but still tethered to, legislatures) typical of government rulemaking.

To say that many of the decisions made by private governance bodies are largely technical is a weak defense. As Giandomenico Majone and others have made clear, technical decisions made in the policy realm are likely to be not purely technical but rather trans-scientific, meaning that they require a high degree of expertise and also entail value choices that experts are in no better position—and have less right—to make than do democratic representatives of a broad electorate.[19] In fact, experts are likely to display a high degree of epistemic bias, a form of intellectual blindness created by their specialized professional training. So their strength can also be their weakness.

Perhaps more serious than epistemic bias are the often severe conflicts of interest embedded in private governance. Those with the most to win or lose from a decision made by private groups are the most likely to be the ones doing the deciding, not merely influencing the decision.

Another limitation of private governance, and one that should concern the participants themselves, is that bureaucracies both in and out of government tend to take on a life of their own, as Robert Michels argued almost a century ago.[20] Organizational imperatives tend to overtake the group's original purposes. These imperatives, such as an organization's funding sources or the aspirations of its managers, can take precedence over members' wishes. Without the equivalent of an independent inspector general, congressional and presidential oversight, an accountability office, or an aware and vigilant public—all of which operate with varying degrees of effectiveness in democratic representative governments—a sharp disjunction between principals (those whom the organization is to serve) and agent (the serving organization) is a predictable result.[21]

That private governance is democratically and even organizationally deficient while significantly affecting the lives of those who are subject to its decisions is sufficient reason for defenders of a free democratic society to be wary of this form of policymaking, even if it is generally accepted and constitutionally protected. Nevertheless, with this book we aim not to condemn private governance but to shine a bright light on it, to recognize it as a category of public policymaking, to advocate that it should be studied on a par with government policymaking, to examine the blemishes that mark private governance, to consider ways to obviate its democratic deficiencies and, where appropriate, to defend it. The goal is to *recognize* private governance, to understand it in its multiple forms, and to make the case that excluding it from the field of public policy diminishes both the understanding of the full policymaking universe and the proper reach of democratic aspirations.

Two

PRIVATE POLICYMAKING: ORIGINS, GROWTH, AND SCOPE

The practice of private organizations making public policy has roots in the distant past, before representative governments were established. Private governance dates back to the Middle Ages when merchants and craft persons in Europe formed associations, often called guilds, that set standards, made regulations, taught apprentices, and provided advice to members. Such guilds were challenged and in some instances supported in their policymaking by ruling elites. Historically, private groups have relied on their expertise to help them establish monopoly control and dominate their policy areas.[1]

In *Seeing Like a State,* James C. Scott examines the development of formal governance over several centuries.[2] He notes that the growth of the state, first for administrative purposes and later to ensure greater fairness, required the development and implementation of standards. Before a state could tax, for example, it had to have a standard of wealth or income upon which to base the tax. Defining property by standards such as hectares, woodlands by cords, and cloth by bolts gave the state a basis for assessing and taxing wealth. Fairness demanded equal treatment; standards provided for it. Those early standards often were borrowed from private sources, including guilds. Just as governments adopted private standards for their own purposes, the public relied on standards to ensure that the products on offer met their needs, and, foreshadowing present practices, the guild members benefited from limiting the numbers of craft persons in competition with one another.

As important as official certification of the authenticity of physical goods was to the public, it became even more necessary as services took on greater economic importance. However, because many aspects of a service go unseen by the consumer, the quality of services rendered is more difficult to evaluate than that of standardized goods. The need to distinguish charlatans and incompetents from qualified professionals in services facilitated the development, by the nineteenth century, of groups that sought to identify and certify appropriately educated service providers. Gradually, national professional organizations, such as the American Medical Association (AMA) and the American Bar Association (ABA), gained dominance in their fields. Such groups and their affiliates established educational and related qualifications for medical and legal practitioners anywhere in the United States, and today they enjoy a major role, respectively, in medical and legal policymaking.[3]

THE MODERN NEED FOR EXPERTISE

As the modern state arose and national economies developed, the need for common standards in products and services grew. Doing business across localities and regions required harmonizing techniques, technologies, and practices, as Marc Olshan explains:

> It wasn't until technological innovation created the potential for
> a truly national economy that the need for formally organized
> standardization activities developed. For example, the efficient

integration of the country's numerous railroads led to the grudging adoption of a standard gauge track in 1886 and standardized automatic couplers and air brakes in 1893. . . . This early rationalization effort was endorsed and to some degree coordinated by two early trade organizations, the American Railway Association . . . and the Master Car Builders Association. . . . The founding of an early professional association, the American Society of Mechanical Engineers in 1880, provided an additional forum for standardizing nomenclature, testing procedures, and hardware.[4]

As economies were nationalizing, Western governments were gradually democratizing. The growth of representative democracies over the past two centuries changed policymaking processes and political power relationships dramatically. Public policy was to be made by those elected to serve the public. Yet the need for help from unelected experts increased as managing and governing the modern state became more complicated. Elected legislators and executives found that, in some areas, they lacked the technical training to develop policy with the specificity necessary to effectively implement the laws they had passed.

In the United States, one response to this difficulty was to increase the technical staff of congressional committees and create legislative agencies, such as the Congressional Research Service and the Government Accountability Office, to provide information to members of Congress.[5] Many large states have followed suit.

However, legislators also found that they needed unelected experts in administrative agencies to fill in the practical details of policy. Delegation to agencies, of course, is not new, but the degree of delegation and the depth of expertise provided are. A classic example of early delegation in the United States dates to the period immediately after the Revolutionary War. Congress entrusted authority for setting and administering veterans' benefits first to the secretary of the Treasury

FIGURE 2-1. *Number of Bills Enacted by Congress in Each Two-Year Term, 1973–2014*

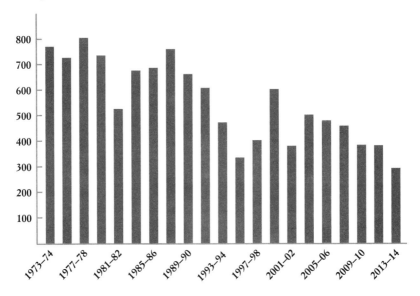

Source: See govtrack.us, "Statistics and Historical Comparison," at www.gov track.us/congress/bills/statistics.

and in 1818 to the secretary of war.[6] In other words, determining the qualifications for benefits and who met those qualifications was left to an administrative agency. The reliance on agency officials to work out the elements of implementation accelerated in the twentieth century during the Progressive Era and then in the wake of the New Deal. It is important to note that agency rules have the force of law. The Supreme Court has largely accepted the practice of extensive delegation to federal administrative agencies, which were making more law than Congress by the end of the twentieth century, as evidenced in a comparison of figure 2-1 above and table 2-1 below.[7]

Agencies, in turn, have increasingly found that they cannot create and enforce appropriate rules without help from experts outside of government. Even with the development of advisory committees and negotiated rulemaking procedures—innovations that infuse more on-

TABLE 2-1. *Total Number of Final Administrative Rules Published, 1997–2012*

Calendar year	Number of final rules	Calendar year	Number of final rules
1997	3,930	2005	3,301
1998	4,388	2006	3,065
1999	4,336	2007	2,947
2000	4,079	2008	3,085
2001	3,423	2009	3,471
2002	3,559	2010	3,260
2003	3,744	2011	3,835
2004	3,661	2012	2,482

Source: Maeve P. Carey, *Counting Regulations: An Overview of Rulemaking, Types of Federal Regulations, and Pages in the Federal Register* (Washington, D.C.: Congressional Research Service 7-5700, 2013), at http://fas.org/sgp/crs/misc/R43056.pdf.

the-ground expertise into agency rulemaking—federal, state, and local governments have turned to private groups for needed expertise.[8]

Three other considerations, beyond expertise, have stimulated the growing reliance on private groups to develop policy. First is the need to convince the business community to recognize new constraints as legitimate and comply with them. For example, when President Franklin D. Roosevelt chose the first commissioner of the U.S. Securities and Exchange Commission (SEC), he named a leading capitalist, Joseph P. Kennedy Sr., thus quelling some of Wall Street's apprehension about government regulation. In turn, the SEC decided that accounting rules would be established by a privately formed and controlled group that evolved into the Financial Accounting Standards Board (FASB).[9] As a result, these crucial decisions were to be left to the "experts." Using the private sector to make and implement standards was intended to

BOX 2-1. *Achieving Perceived Fairness and Avoiding*
Blame: The Case of Demand Exceeding Supply
of Human Organs for Transplantation

In 1984, Congress established the Organ Procurement and Transplantation Network (OPTN). The National Organ Transplant Act called
for a unified transplant network to be operated by a private, non-profit
organization under federal contract. The United Network for Organ
Sharing (UNOS) was awarded the initial OPTN contract on September 30, 1986, and has continued to administer the OPTN since that
time under the overall purview of the Department of Health and
Human Services. As is evident, who gets an organ, among the many
patients in need, is several steps removed from Congress, which assigned responsibility for allocating organs far beyond its aegis. As a
result, a member of Congress with a constituent whose teenager
desperately needs a liver can say to the distressed parent, "This
matter is out of my control. UNOS makes the rules." Removing political sway in such a matter seems fair but also makes it impossible for

promote acceptance and compliance among businesses. Today, the SEC
follows a related theory of compliance when it relies on companies to
investigate themselves if the SEC perceives possible wrongdoing. In
health and safety standards, government bodies often rely on self-
reporting and self-disclosure at the first level of enforcement.[10]

A second reason for increasing dependence on private groups is
that elected politicians would rather not make unpopular policies that
lose them votes at the polls. When lawmakers see the need to resolve
a contentious problem but do not want their records tainted by voting
for a painful solution, one option, political scientist Douglas Arnold
has argued, is not to leave their fingerprints on the policy, thereby
making electoral retribution next to impossible.[11] This tactic was followed, for example, in the 1983 Social Security Act Amendments,
which in effect increased the Social Security tax by extending the age

the constituent to blame the Congress member for failing to save the loved one.

Separating representative government from rules made by an independent organization can be a good idea to ensure fair, non-preferential allocation of organs. However, one cannot simply assume that rulemaking by an outside group is necessarily fair, and the public needs to know what is necessary to change the rules when they do not work appropriately. For example, Zink and colleagues found in 2005 that UNOS's policies "enable those on the list with the proper resources to gain an advantage over other less fortunate members, creating a system that benefits not the individual most in medical need, but the one with the best resources."[a]

a. S. Zink, S. S. Wertlieb, J. Calano, and V. Matwin, "Examining the Potential Exploitation of UNOS Policies," *American Journal of Bioethics* 5, no. 4 (2005): 6–10. For a positive overview of the history of OPTN, and its agility and competence in comparison with either public or for-profit agencies, see David L. Weimer, *Medical Governance: Values, Expertise, and Interests in Organ Transplantation* (Georgetown University Press, 2010).

of eligibility for full benefits from sixty-five to sixty-seven. This extension would not take place, however, for many years after the vote. Most members of Congress present when the change was instituted would no longer be in office when the impact of the provision was felt. Moreover, with both political parties cooperating on this reform, neither could be tagged as the culprit for increasing the retirement age should voters notice.

Politicians are by necessity credit-takers not blame-accepters.[12] David Weimer's review of fourth-arena, hybrid government institutions cites blame avoidance as a central reason for creating these strange amalgams.[13] Perhaps the best example among private governance bodies can be found in the structure created by Congress to allocate human organs for transplant to address the problem of demand greatly exceeding supply, as illustrated in box 2-1.

Third, the burgeoning dependence on private groups to make rules and administer public programs is part of a larger trend toward relying on private groups to do what could be seen as the government's work. Starting with President Jimmy Carter's move in the late 1970s to eliminate costly and anti-competitive governmental regulations—for example in interstate commerce and domestic airline fare-setting—a sea change began in American politics and swelled under President Ronald Reagan. Reagan and his allies on Capitol Hill strongly asserted the view that big government was inefficient, wasteful, and too expensive, and that regulations were counterproductive.

Their solution was to cut taxes, reduce federal employment, contract out to private businesses and nonprofits where possible, eliminate duplicative programs, remove what they perceived as burdensome regulations, and take related measures to reverse course. Civilian employment in federal government was cut in half (in absolute numbers) to fewer than 1 million workers, while the number of government-contractor employees multiplied from 194,500 in 1993 to more than 2.3 million in 2012.[14] The reliance on private governance groups to make and enforce rules fits nicely into this new governance model of privatization, even though private governance is not coterminous with privatization as it is usually understood.

WHAT IS PRIVATIZATION?

Dividing "privatization" into three distinct elements helps to unpack this concept, remove some of the confusion that surrounds its use, and clarify exactly where private governance fits into it.

First, the word can be used to denote a shift to the private sector in administering publicly funded goods and services. Government generates and pays for these activities. The private entities contracted to perform public services may be for-profit corporations such as Lockheed-Martin and Bechtel Corp., whose primary goal is to increase stockholder value, or nonprofits such as the Red Cross and Catholic Charities, which are committed to their missions and their own survival. In determining whether contracting out to such groups is appropriate, the most important question to ask is: To what degree are the private groups' goals consistent with government's goals in contracting out its work? To ensure that objectives are properly aligned, government officials must have sufficient expertise and resources to write tight contracts and oversee their execution, and contractors must be given incentives to ensure that they deliver the highest quality work from the government's point of view.[15] When people talk about privatization, they are usually referring to this meaning.

A second meaning is the complete removal of government from an activity—including funding, implicit guarantees against liabilities, or any sort of government imprimatur. For example, people who argue for privatizing Fannie Mae, a fourth-arena entity that creates the main secondary market for home mortgages, want Fannie Mae to become a truly private corporation and the federal government, in effect, to get out of the mortgage business by ceasing to back Fannie Mae. When a country privatizes an industry such as oil production, the government's oil monopoly is eliminated, and the industry is opened to the vagaries of market competition.

A third possible meaning of privatization, usually either unrecognized for its importance or thoughtlessly lumped into the general category of privatization, is private governance. This third element is consistent with the overall trend of relying more on the private sector, which, proponents argue, is more efficient, cheaper, and faster than relying on government agencies, which are burdened by red tape. As Arthur Okun has argued, however, in most cases what is gained in efficiency necessarily entails a loss in fairness and democratic control.[16] Moreover, self-regulation is not necessarily more efficient, as the economic debacle of 2007–08 demonstrates. Nor is it cheaper; instead, regulatory costs are shifted to private sector groups and ultimately hidden, as the public has no idea what private governance costs or who is paying in the last instance. In any case, pitting private governance against public governance is an uneven contest. Remove the red tape and the constitutional necessities of separation of powers, deliberations open to the public, representative government and the Bill of Rights, and government could be equally efficient. Of course, such an enterprise would no longer constitute government of, by, and for the people, and it would not be fair. The Founders chose representation, protection from tyranny, and democratic values over efficiency. Since the late 1970s, that choice seems to have dimmed.

WHY PRIVATE GROUPS SUPPORT
PRIVATE GOVERNANCE

While governments have found it necessary to rely on private policymaking groups for their expertise and experience, the groups themselves have several reasons to encourage governments to rely on them. Government regulation of their areas can be cumbersome, time-consuming, expensive, and sometimes, inefficient from an industry perspective. It hardly needs to be said that they prefer "self-regulation" to government regulation.

Furthermore, private policymakers want to control the content of the rules under which they operate. When they face conflicts of interest between increasing firm and industry profits and creating fair rules for all, profits are likely to trump fairness.[17] They can, for instance, create barriers to keep new enterprises from entering the industry, barriers that both government and market forces would otherwise discourage.[18] There are numerous examples of excessively stringent rules made by insiders to control the number of newcomers or limit competition within a profession. Such rules are often justified in the name of maintaining high quality.[19] Alternatively, private governance bodies can choose the opposite route, making rules that are much more accommodating to businesses than government would have made and thus are more welcome than government regulation.

Another attraction of private policymaking to those who engage in it is that courts legitimize their rules—and make them predictable—as industry standards. For example, following established industry standards, even those not adopted or made by government, can reduce a firm's legal liability when accidents occur. Alternatively, a company may be found liable for an injury when it does not follow privately made safety standards, a fact that reinforces the authority of private rulemakers. (See box 2-2 for one example of this practice.) Although law takes precedence over private policies, litigants can point to private standards to defend or support their actions when no relevant law or regulation pertains.[20]

Through the mechanism of private governance, private groups are not just passive takers of rules but proactive makers of the rules of the game they play. The economic, political, and social benefits of setting and implementing public rules are obviously enormous, and without an appropriate and carefully designed channel for public and civic engagement, those benefits are in the hands of private groups themselves.

It is true that sometimes private actors can unite and successfully address a problem. As Elinor Ostrom has famously demonstrated, when there is a common resource that must be shared, like a body of water, the actors directly affected can come together, without government, and make reasonable decisions.[21] Self-organized governance can and does work, as industry self-regulation shows, particularly for the industry. However, the question here is one of democratic accountability to a larger public. Can organizational forms that do not rely on command-and-control mechanisms work? Ostrom shows that for one category of problems—those related to managing common pool resources—they can, and remarkably her solution is scalable. Others have suggested that co-regulation (a combination of government and self-regulation) can be both effective and accountable to a larger public.[22] And still others who

BOX 2-2. *Example: A Finding of Partial Liability on the Grounds of Not Adhering to Private Standards*

In January 1991, approximately two weeks after he was hired, a man started working as a tilt pot operator in the factory. Tilt pot operation, a job which was previously performed by highly-trained veterans with more than 10 years of experience in the factory, involves the use of electronic controls to transfer "ingots"—long rolls of aluminum heated to approximately 900 degrees Fahrenheit—from large pots to a moving conveyor system. The conveyor system is called the "hotline" and is used to transport the ingots throughout the factory. In addition to tilting the pots, the [worker's] job required him to climb on to the hotline periodically to measure the temperature of the ingots. Less than one month after the [employee] was hired, his leg was amputated following a work accident. The [worker] had climbed onto the hotline to check temperatures and another inexperienced employee inadvertently changed the direction of the conveyor causing the man's leg to be crushed by one of the moving ingots. The designer of the conveyor system and former owner of the company, Kaiser Aluminum and Chemical Corp., was found partially liable for the employee's injury for not designing the conveyor system according to accepted private industry safety standards despite its contention that the standards were not mandatory.

Source: Michelle Ranville, "The Effectiveness of Participation in Public and Private Standard Setting," Ph.D. dissertation, George Mason University, 2014, p. 2. Case cited: *Stone* v. *United Engineering, a Division of Wean, Inc.,* 197 W. Va. 347, 475 S.E.2d 439 (1996).

are concerned about public inclusion in decisionmaking also answer in the affirmative if new designs in governance are developed.[23]

PRIVATE GOVERNANCE GROUPS ENTANGLED
WITH GOVERNMENT

Private governance groups rely on government for much more than its courts. A standard-setting organization such as UL, an independent, for-profit group financed by manufacturers, writes rules on product safety and then certifies products that meet them. Products that fail are unlikely to be sold in U.S. or foreign markets.[24] UL decisions directly affect free markets, and in most respects, UL operates like a government regulator. In fact, a federal regulatory agency, the Occupational Safety and Health Administration (OSHA), has formally approved UL's work, relying on and certifying it as if it were OSHA's own.[25]

Another example of the complex—both conflicting and complementary—relationships between government agencies and private standards-setters is the case of the National Institute of Standards and Technology (NIST) and the American National Standards Institute. A private, nonprofit corporation, ANSI accredits voluntary consensus standards developed by standards-developing organizations.[26] For reasons of clarity, one might think of ANSI (and similar groups described later) as an "uber" or "peak" organization in that its members are other organizations. ANSI is not a standard-creating organization in itself but an organization that sets down the rules its member standard-setting groups must follow to continue to be ANSI members and to create American National Standards.

ANSI covers more than 200 standards developers and more than 10,000 American National Standards (ANS). Its stated goal is to enhance the "global competitiveness of U.S. business and the American quality of life," yet ANSI is a private corporation "free from centralized government control."[27] This idea, asserted on ANSI's website, is "firmly rooted in American history," apparently an oblique reference to the fact that ANSI elbowed out the federal government's Bureau of Standards (NIST today) as the predominant standard-setter early in the twentieth century. NIST now plays a subordinate and peripheral role in the standardization system while ANSI has achieved its legitimacy as an official "quasi-governmental" accreditation organization.[28] ANSI ambiguously concedes, however, that the private infrastructure is "strengthened through governmental participation," the precise dimensions of which are left unspecified.[29]

An example of the powerful position taken by ANSI in public policymaking is its close collaboration with OSHA on worker safety. Much of OSHA's work in the two years immediately after its founding in 1971 consisted of using industry consensus standards as the bases for OSHA standards, which then became law. In this way, standards and rules written by a private organization became part of the regulatory framework. For OSHA standards promulgated pursuant to § (6)(b) of the OSH Act, the secretary of labor is required under § (6)(b)(8), whenever a rule differs substantially from a national consensus standard, to state the reasons the rule as adopted will better effectuate the purposes of the act than the national consensus standard.[30] OMB Circular A-119, mentioned in chapter 1, ordered that industry consensus safety standards be the basis for OSHA regulation.[31] In other words, OSHA must demonstrate that government regulation would be more effective than the consensus standards at improving safety.[32]

As these examples of the intermingling of government and private governance show, the source of requirements imposed on citizens can be difficult to trace, and they are likely to favor those who participate in making the rules. As ANSI explains, "the U.S. standardization system reflects a market-driven and highly diversified society," but few people understand how this system works and affects them. That OSHA is compelled to serve ANSI demonstrates the governmental agency's fundamental weakness and the private group's dominance of public policymaking in standardization.

Without the help of nongovernmental policymakers, the size and nature of public policy challenges likely would have grown beyond governments' ability to handle them. In responding to the forces of increasing complexity, governments have two choices. They can hire more experts or they can rely on private groups to supply that expertise. Governments have done both. But the available evidence suggests that the need for nongovernment policymakers will continue to grow.[33]

GLOBALIZATION AND EXPANSION
OF PRIVATE GOVERNANCE

It is a truism that an integrated and interconnected world requires coordination if markets are to thrive and public health and welfare in particular are to be protected. Perhaps the most glaring recent examples of this need come from the 2007–08 global financial meltdown and the deadly Ebola outbreak in 2014 in West Africa that threatened to spread throughout the world with potentially catastrophic consequences. Clearly, many of the same imperatives that led to national rulemaking have shifted to the international and transnational level.[34] However, a global governance gap exists with too few state-led, internationally authoritative rulemakers to deal with such crises.[35]

When governments fail to act, the field is open to private actors to make rules themselves.[36] Private actors can include a wide range of organizations: multi-stakeholder groups such as the Extractive Industries Transparency Initiative to fight corruption and the World Commission on Dams to create dam-building guidelines; industries whose members collaborate to establish technical standards to ensure interconnectivity and increase business opportunities; professionals who create common accounting methods; insurers that determine which ships are seaworthy; and corporations such as Nestlé and Wal-Mart that enforce specific health and safety rules for their suppliers.[37] Sometimes the decisions of these groups are determinative in that if a company wants to do business internationally (or with a dominant multinational corporation), it must follow the standards set, with little or no say in the matter.

In other cases, groups compete to establish rules, leaving businesses to choose which ones to follow (usually the cheapest and most convenient) and resulting in confusion for the consumer.[38] For example, it is anybody's guess what "fair-trade" or "organic" really means, as definitions abound. Confusingly, the American Tree Farm System (ATFS), the Forest Stewardship Council (FSC), and the Sustainable Forestry Initiative (SFI) all certify that the lumber a homeowner buys at the hardware store has been handled in an environmentally sensitive manner along the supply chain, from forest to manufacturer to retailer. However, the FSC's standards are much more rigorous and comprehensive (including serious labor and GMO standards) than those of the industry-created Forest Industry Council.[39] How is the average end-user to know the difference? Moreover, an Internet search for lumber certification standards reveals that the industry's case for its position is much more prominently displayed and much easier to find than that of the apparently more balanced FSC.

How nongovernmental or private groups fit into global public policymaking and how the increased level of activity of private governance affects representative governments is far from settled. Is the authority of nation-states being undermined or circumvented by private rules? Under what circumstances might the use of private rules be a good or bad development? Is the public's influence attenuated or even eliminated as the chain of representation lengthens from citizen to legislature to public bureaucracy to domestic private governance to transnational private governance?[40] Still, short of a massive global disaster, transnational coordination will be increasingly needed; and for a variety of reasons, the locus of decisionmaking will not be exclusively within and controlled by sovereign states.

Not least, international bodies (with nations making the decisions) tend to have cumbersome operating rules, are slow to act, and are characterized by bureaucratic lethargy.[41] Beyond time-consuming inefficiency, significant interests may not be best represented through

BOX 2-3. *An Annual Greeting from the International Organization for Standardization, an Organization with Members in 165 Countries*

Happy World Standards Day!

Every year, we celebrate World Standards Day on 14 October to pay tribute to the thousands of experts who share their know-how and expertise to develop International Standards.

You may not be aware of it: every day, wherever you go, there is a hidden but fascinating world of standards around you, helping out with everything you do. Don't believe me? Take a peak into this person's morning journey and you will be surprised. There are standards for nearly everything, from coffee to watches, from dental floss to bicycles. Every day is truly a standards journey!

In 2014 we recognize the efforts of all those who, through standards, "level the playing field", simplifying and enhancing life. Countries that have mainstreamed International Standards in their policies and regulations are able to better protect their populations and give them a bigger choice of quality products from around the globe. They also give industry the opportunity to enter new markets, boosting our economies. International Standards are good for everyone, from the largest to the smallest players such as small and medium-sized enterprises, who will find it easier to access technological know-how and best practice, and compete internationally.

Source: International Organization for Standardization, at www.iso.org/iso /home/news_index/news_archive/news.htm?refid=ref1898.

the state-centric system, as the United Nations has recognized with its system of registering nonvoting NGOs (nongovernmental organizations) involved in issues taken up by the international body.

However, several difficulties arise in creating and maintaining arrangements outside of international bodies where sovereign nations come together, agree on rules, and enforce them. Transnational governance groups lack the legitimacy heretofore enjoyed by the state, or, by extension, by intergovernmental bodies established via formal treaties. Further, transnational entities have little ability at the outset to impel obedience to the rules set or to enforce compliance. Without that ability, they inevitably encounter the quintessential collective action problems of shirking and free-riding on the part of some member-participants.[42] As private governance groups monopolize their areas of expertise (proverbially becoming "the only game in town"), the companies wanting to do business in those areas may have no choice but to comply.

Transnational groups such as the International Organization for Standardization are thriving and celebrate their success (see box 2-3). However, even to imagine workable transnational governance that meets basic democratic standards seems beyond human abilities.[43]

Transnational bodies that have a monopoly on creating standards, especially in a technical area such as the multi-stakeholder Internet Corporation for Assigned Names and Numbers (ICANN), have the best chance of inducing global cooperation and coordination.[44] They also make distributive decisions in which most people have no say. In order to work, the domain name system of the Internet for which ICANN is responsible must be a monopoly. Telecommunication companies have no alternatives to the scheme set out by ICANN and hence are compelled to follow it. At the same time, a valiant effort to allow interested persons everywhere to participate in selecting representatives to sit on the ICANN board of directors failed utterly.[45]

To better understand the vast world of private governance organizations, it will be helpful to examine some subject-matter areas and a few of the bodies operating in them. First, however, we turn to the grounds on which to assess private governance, with a primary focus on questions of public control.

Three

HOW TO ASSESS PRIVATE GOVERNANCE

Judging the merits and demerits of private governance means agreeing on criteria for evaluating such groups and their policymaking activities. On one hand are the questions to which the hoped-for answer is yes: Is the group accountable beyond its own constituency? Do its policies facilitate the proper functioning of free markets, improve public welfare, promote the social trust on which peaceful societies rely, and positively supplement governmental regulation? On the other hand are the questions to which the answer ought to be no: Do its rulemaking procedures differ significantly from those followed by government agencies? Do its rules encourage industry or professional self-dealing? Are public interests placed at the forefront of decisions? Underlying all of these questions, however, is the more foundational one of legitimacy. Is private governance a legitimate form of rulemaking and rule-imposing?

LEGITIMACY OF GOVERNING INSTITUTIONS

An institution establishes its legitimacy on moral grounds. What right has it to exist and to make rules that must be followed by others? With their theories of social contract, Thomas Hobbes and John Locke sought to authenticate the existence of government—a harsh government that maintains peace (Hobbes) and representative government (Locke). Modernity has embraced Locke over Hobbes, democracy over dictatorship.

For a classic statement of illegitimate government, look no further than the Declaration of Independence, which disavows Britain's rule over the American colonies, asserts the "inalienable rights" of every person to submit (or not) to public authority, and defines the limits of legitimate government. The Preamble to the Constitution of the United States goes on to establish the legitimacy of the new American government. Both of these sources are worth reviewing to see the kinds of normative defenses that underlie the claims of legitimacy for republican self-government. In general, public institutions (as opposed to the family, for example) are said to be legitimate if they are sufficiently democratic, even if the democracy is indirect and representative.[1]

But normative justification, no matter how compelling, is inadequate to establish and maintain legitimate institutions. They must follow procedures that lend credence to their right to rule, their decisions must be accepted voluntarily by most people, and their governance must be effective.[2]

The specific procedures put in place by legitimate institutions vary, but they follow from democratic principles and can be assessed empirically. Typically, such principles include (1) transparency in institutions' structure, procedures, decisions, and reasoning;[3] (2) inclusiveness regarding the ideas, concerns, and material interests of those affected by their decisions; and (3) accountability, which requires decisionmakers to be answerable for the way decisions are made and the substance of the results.[4] It should be clear that a democratically legitimate institution must include and be accountable to—and thus accessible to—those in whose name it acts, and it must be transparent in its activities. Among these qualities, perhaps nothing is more central to legitimate governance than accountability.

ACCOUNTABILITY

Among the many ways to conceive of accountability in the context of private governance, five approaches seem most relevant. Most simply, accountability can be seen, first, as giving an account to someone or being entrusted to carry out a task and held responsible for a specific outcome. In this sense, accountability is after the fact, essentially punitive or sanction-bearing. Put differently, a principal (or a person with ultimate authority in a given situation) delegates authority to an agent to perform one or more duties on behalf of and in the interest of the principal.[5] Accountability in this case asks how the principal can be sure that the agent has performed these duties properly.

The principal-agent concept focuses on the possible slippage between the principal and the agent. The principal cannot know every detail of what the agent does, and inherently the agent's interest will not be identical to that of the principal. This informational asymmetry, coupled with divergent interests, is known as the principal-agent problem. Complicating the situation further, an agent might be, and often is, answerable to multiple principals who do not have identical interests.[6] In these circumstances, perfect accountability cannot be achieved even theoretically. However, agents can be removed, for example, if principals are dissatisfied with their results.

Political theorist Jane Mansbridge argues that after-the-fact accountability is inefficient.[7] The principal loses: the outcome is unsatisfactory, the agent is fired, and the principal must start all over again. Or, a deceitful agent can hide actions that are not in the principal's interest, and hence the principal is ill-served. How much better it would be, she argues, if the agent wanted to serve the principal, with the result that the interests of the two are properly aligned. A proper congruence of their interests constitutes before-the-fact accountability, which she calls a "selection model," a second way to consider this concept. In other words, the principal-agent relationship is underpinned by trust. More time is spent identifying the right agents in the first place. In this model, the principal knows what to expect of a professionally trained agent, the agent knows how to perform professionally, and neither monitoring nor sanctions are needed. Instead accountability occurs via deliberation and discussion. A lawyer as agent, for example, serves the interest of her client because she wants to, believes she ought to, knows how to, has sincerely promised to do so, and, for Mansbridge, discusses her actions with the client. The lawyer's interests are subordinate to those of the client. In the same way, surgeons, engineers, professors, and other professionals can avoid conflicts of interest or other compromising situations by adopting appropriate ethical standards of practice.

Political philosopher Jon Elster points out, however, that as valuable as professional expectations may be, norms are relatively weak in the face of temptation.[8] One temptation may be created by the market system. When professionals practice as proprietors or employees or are rewarded for holding down costs, for example by insurers who pay for their services, making money or keeping their jobs might be a higher priority than following all professional precepts. Professionals today typically have multiple principals—their professions, businesses, superiors, third-party payers—whose expectations conflict. This clash highlights the nearly untenable situation in which professionals are often placed in a market system.

Thus, as helpful and efficient as undistorted, before-the-fact (or belief-in-professional-standards or the selection model of) accountability may be, it probably needs to be supplemented by after-the-fact accountability, as Mansbridge recognizes. Mansbridge's important contribution is to point out that accountability need not be conceived exclusively as punitive and that trust between principals and agents can be engendered.[9] For our purposes here, consider the private-governance example of professionals who make rules that affect those outside the profession (see also chapter 6). The questions to ask are: To what degree are such practitioners answerable to their professions to practice at the highest practical and ethical levels possible? Or are they more beholden to market pressures or to employers and payers and therefore likely to underperform or to misrepresent?

Like professions that require rigorous training, most forms of private governance seem to need after-the-fact accountability. How might that be attained? Legal theorist Jerry Mashaw offers a third perspective.[10] He suggests that accountability is contextual and provides six questions that can help define accountability in a particular situation: "accountability to whom? by whom? about what? through what processes? by what standards? and with what effect?" Together these questions can be applied to what he calls an "accountability regime." A regime is an arrangement of people and institutions interacting in a domain in which some people are answerable to others. One regime might be private governance, which then can be compared with other regimes (such as those of government agencies or legislatures) with regard to public expectations for their performance, their different capabilities, and the possibilities for a hybrid regime (combining governmental and private elements) that might produce a better institutional design.[11] As we discuss the examples of private policymaking in the fields of finance, food safety, and the professions in this book, these six questions should be in the foreground in assessing the legitimacy of private governance.

A fourth way to consider accountability, and in particular democratic accountability, is from the perspective of representation. In their superb book *Representation,* Mónica Brito Vieira and David Runciman treat representation as a foundational concept in democracy and in other principal-agent situations, and as a concept on which accountability rests.[12] To untangle the often complex responsibilities entailed in the act of representation, they use the idea of a chain of representation. It should be possible to chart the connections between principal and agent and among principals and agents. In a representative democracy, the principal is the citizen and the agent the elected official. In a private, self-governing organization such as a garden club, the American Bankers Association (in most of its activities), or the Sierra Club, the principals are the group's members (though the members are not necessarily equals, as in the case of the American Bankers Association, in which larger banks carry more weight).

Sometimes the chain includes intervening principals and agents, yielding a complicated set of obligations that can ultimately dissolve the chain. For instance, an organization such as the private International Organization of Securities Commissions (IOSCO), discussed briefly in the next chapter, is composed of securities officials from many countries. Following the chain of representation from national citizens—in whose interest commissioners presumably operate—to the decisions made at IOSCO is almost impossible.[13] As the chain lengthens, possible distortions in carrying out (or even knowing) the will of the principal multiply. If the starting point in a democracy is the public, what is one to make of a private group composed of government officials making public policy? If the starting point is not the public, how can a private governance group be legitimate in its role as public policymaker?

This chain-of-representation concept is particularly useful in evaluating efforts to close the global governance gap by creating private institutions to solve public problems. For example, a group such as the International Commission on Dams is composed of the major stakeholders in dam building; among these stakeholders are environmental NGOs, representatives who in turn are said to represent the public.[14] Which public? How? To whom are these representatives accountable? Through what processes? And so on. Often groups such as the independent Financial Industry Regulatory Authority (FINRA), which is the largest securities regulator in the United States, include "public representatives" on their boards. In FINRA the majority of board members are public. How and by whom are those representatives selected? For whom are those representatives standing? How does the representative know what the public, or a particular public, wants? Is the public even aware that it has "public representatives" on this body? Is a "public representative" held accountable in any way? Mashaw's six questions seem particularly relevant in trying to follow a chain of representation. Clearly, much work needs to be done to clarify and investigate the relationship between "public" and "public representative."

Fifth, accountability may focus on procedure.[15] Does the group follow specified democratic practices, and does it consistently follow a rule of law—constitutional and statutory for government groups, bylaws and procedural agreements for private governance groups? One set of procedural requirements for public agencies operating under powers delegated by an elected legislature and chief executive is set forth in the 1946 Administrative Procedure Act (APA), as amended.[16] These processes, while often cumbersome, could be considered the gold standard of democratic rulemaking in several ways. The chain of representation, though indirect, clearly leads back to the general public. The principles that underlie the APA constitute the essential elements of democratic practice: transparency, inclusiveness, and accountability. Specifically, the APA requires: adequate notice and extensive justification for proposed changes to rules; considered deliberation; opportunity for public participation; responsiveness to objections to a rule raised by any member of the public; publication of the rule, which is then freely available to and easily accessible by the public; and an appeals process within the agency and through the courts. Elected officials guide the process; the president can block the rule; and Congress can prohibit use of public funds to implement it.[17] Because agencies are part of the government, they are further subject to the requirements of the Freedom of Information Act (FOIA) under most circumstances, making it difficult for them to hide their actions from the press or the public. Constitutional strictures, too, apply to the work of government agencies.

Should private governance institutions be held to such exacting standards of democratic legitimacy? Some of the organizations themselves seem conflicted about this question, and answers vary. Groups that include a "public" member, permit public comment on their proposals, or freely publish their decisions appear to endorse some aspects of inclusiveness and transparency. ANSI, the private organization of policymaking groups, requires that its members follow many of the practices of the federal government's Administrative Procedure Act, demonstrating that it recognizes the public nature of its enterprise and hence some of the obligations of publicness. However, Michelle Ranville closely compared ANSI's procedures with those of the federal rulemaking process and demonstrated that ANSI's are not equivalent to or as stringent as those of the government.[18] A particularly troublesome difference is that ANSI and its accredited rulemaking groups sell their standards, making them far from freely available to the public. (See table 3-1 for Ranville's point-by-point comparison.) For those private governance groups in the form of for-profit corporations, APA-type requirements simply do not fit how they operate.[19]

The key to determining whether independent policymaking groups should adhere to democratic principles is the degree to which private institutions function as public ones. If a group's activities dictate the health and welfare of those outside the group, even if it is legally incorporated as private, standards of democratic legitimacy should apply. However, private governance groups can and do use their legal structure to conceal what they do and to limit what the public can know about their processes and decisions. They are not subject to APA or FOIA requirements. Sometimes it is impossible to find out how they operate. For-profit and not-for-profit corporations—the legal personalities private governance groups take on—have rights to privacy, to protect their proprietary property (including their rules), and to keep private the names of their members. The U.S. Supreme Court has strengthened corporate rights in recent years by expanding the concept of corporations as persons, most dramatically in the area of contributions to political campaigns.[20] Such rights, however, conflict with fundamental precepts of public governance: of, by, and for the people. As a practical matter, however, private groups take up much of the governance space and can serve important public purposes. Recognizing this reality raises the question of what the public should expect of private governance groups, what constraints should be placed on them, and how to increase their democratic legitimacy.

GOVERNMENT CANNOT DO EVERYTHING: SOME ADVANTAGES OF PRIVATE GOVERNANCE

While private governance might lack a sufficient normative justification, it can have some practical advantages. For example, it can improve market functioning by creating standards for interoperability across technical platforms or in making up-to-date rules that regulate the newest technology. It can fill in where government is nonexistent, for instance, in addressing the global governance gap.[21] It can fill in when the institutions of democratic government fail to perform for one reason or another. It can supplement government regulatory decisions by creating rules that the government subsequently adopts.[22]

As discussed previously, technical, highly scientific rulemaking would seem to be an area especially suited for private governance groups. State-of-the-art technicians and professionals work within industry and in many cases are best equipped to make and amend rules as new technologies arise. The argument is that government cannot keep up. From a technical standpoint, private governance groups are in a position to make the best rules.

This justification points to the effectiveness criterion of legitimacy. It also highlights the acceptance criterion. For example, people accept the decisions of UL, which has become a trusted source of high-quality standards. Why do UL technicians (that is, agents) not raise principal-agent problems for the manufacturers or the public (that is,

TABLE 3-1. *APA and ANSI Procedural Requirements Compared*

	Administrative Procedure Act (requirements apply to U.S. government agencies that develop regulations)	American National Standards Institute (requirements apply to organizations that develop American National Standards [ANS])
	Notice and comment	
Notice time before rule or standard becomes effective	30 days unless agency finds good cause for shorter time [§553(d)(1-3)]	30–60 days depending on the mode of publication. (Sec.2.5.2.)
Content of notice	(1) a statement of the time, place, and nature of rule making proceedings; (2) reference to the legal authority under which the rule is proposed; and (3) either the terms or substance of the proposed rule or a description of the subjects and issues involved.	"Notice should include a clear and meaningful description of the purpose of the proposed activity and shall identify a readily available source for further information." (Sec.2.1)
Access to proposed and final standards	Public has access via the Federal Register [§552(a)(1)(D)]	Any person or group can obtain access to an American National Standards (ANS) by requiring a copy from the developer. Some, but not all, require a fee. Developers determine fees.
Who may submit comments?	"Interested persons" can submit "written data, views, or arguments" to the agency, and the agency "must provide basis and purpose" for issuing the rule in light of relevant comments [§553(c)]	Anyone can submit comments on a proposed standards. There are no rules to govern how SDOs or ANSI must consider submitted comments.

Appeals

Burden of proof	" . . . a defendant shall serve his answer within thirty days after the service of the complaint. The burden is on the defendant to sustain his action." [§552b(h)(1)]	"The burden of proof to show adverse effect [of a standard] shall be on the appellant." (Sec.2.7.1)
Time limit for appeals	Established by each agency. [§552a(f)(4)]	"Appeals of actions shall be made *within reasonable time limits* (emphasis added); appeals of inactions may be made at any time." (Sec.2.7.1)
Who may appeal	"Each agency shall give an interested person the right to petition for the issuance, amendment, or repeal of a rule." [§553(e)] or "any person . . ." on the grounds that the standard did not follow APA procedural requirements for notice and comment. [§552b(g)]	"Persons [with interest] directly and materially affected interests and who have been or will be adversely affected by any procedural action or inaction by a standards developer with regard to the development . . . , revision, reaffirmation, or withdrawal of an existing American National Standard, have the right to appeal." (Sec.2.7.1) To be considered as having a direct and material interest, a person must have commented on a standard when it was proposed or must have been a member of the consensus board.

Source: Michelle Ranville, "The Effectiveness of Participation in Public and Private Standard Setting," Ph.D. dissertation, George Mason University, 2014, p. 48. Content of notice can be found in 5 U.S.C. 553(b).

principals)? One likely answer is that highly trained professionals are making the decisions about what is safe. Their jobs and the public's interest in safe products are aligned. The technicians are not paid to minimize product requirements; they are paid to protect the public from harm. In short, those making the decisions will not have to cope with conflicts of interest—that is, asymmetry between agent and principal. However, since UL is financed by industry, it is hard not to conclude that its first concern is to serve industry.

This example provides a helpful benchmark for assessing private governance when it is engaged in technical, scientific decisionmaking rather than value choices. As Majone has noted, however, individual governance decisions in contemporary society frequently involve *both* technical expertise *and* preferences that are not a question of expertise.[23] One way to consider this matter is to see each decision on a continuum, from technical expertise on one end to value choices on the other. The closer to the value pole, the more the criteria of democratic legitimacy (including significant public involvement) should apply. The closer to the technical expertise pole, the less democrats need to be concerned. Similarly, a continuum can be applied to conflicts of interest. The more the experts' interests diverge from those of the public, the more important democratic legitimacy criteria become. The more the interests of the two are apparently in concert, as in the case of UL, the less the public's involvement in a decision is needed.[24] On this view, the securities regulator FINRA, described more fully in the next chapter, should have much more public involvement than UL. As a private governance institution, UL appears to fulfill the promise of private governance because it provides needed technical expertise with fewer complications and value choices than FINRA. UL begins with an agreed-upon value choice, safety, and then makes technical decisions to reach the safety goal. FINRA's work is much less straightforward.

As the next chapters also discuss, private groups supplement and can be co-opted by, endorsed by, and even created by government. In the area of finance, for example, a decision was made eighty years ago to use existing private bodies to create and enforce rules, in part to get buy-in by the affected industries and practitioners, such as securities dealers and accountants. And when the U.S. government has needed mechanisms to identify institutions of sufficient quality to warrant receipt of public funds, it has turned to preexisting private accrediting organizations to perform and underwrite the work. Much governance work relies on private groups. It would be very difficult for governments in the United States to do their jobs without decisionmaking help from private groups.

Another advantage of private groups—putative but suspect—is that they are more efficient than government. Are they? And if so, are they more efficient because they are not burdened by the procedural rules that democratic bodies must follow—in other words, because they are not held accountable to the same degree as public agencies? Troublesome procedural requirements were established to ensure that agencies produce democratically legitimate rules. Fewer requirements may lead to speedier, but not necessarily better, decisions.

BEYOND DEMOCRATIC LEGITIMACY

In any examination of private governance, what is missing is as important as what exists. Common standards for interoperability or supply-chain consistency, when made by private groups, may be perfectly reasonable. But industry rules tend to benefit the industry, and rules that would help the public at the expense of profits might not be on industry's agenda if maximizing shareholder value is the overriding concern. Some examples: creating interchangeable charger cords for consumer electronics products; establishing consistent mattress ratings across brands to facilitate comparison; establishing frequent-flyer standards so that airlines cannot change the rules of the game in mid-air, so to speak; or devising leg-room, seat-size, and seat-back standards across airlines. Such rules are unlikely to be made by a government that promotes free enterprise, but they could be made by industry groups. The reason industry groups do not make them is clear and points to a deficiency in private governance.

Private governance might also be evaluated on the degree to which it improves the functioning of markets. As the U.S. Supreme Court recognized in 1988, the American Bar Association should not be permitted to prohibit lawyers from advertising their services.[25] Even when the decision is made by a governmentally chartered board such as the North Carolina State Board of Dental Examiners, private agreements in restraint of trade are not permissible.[26] The difficulty lies in determining when such restraint has occurred. Congress has suspended antitrust considerations for cross-firm, consensus-based, standards-setting bodies, though this area of law is fraught with uncertainties.[27]

THE LEAST THE PUBLIC SHOULD DEMAND
OF PRIVATE GOVERNANCE GROUPS

In a perfect world, private governance would be democratically legitimate. Much work needs to be done to sort out how to accomplish this large order. In the interim, some minimum standards of democratic accountability should apply when private groups are making rules that affect the broader public. First, decisionmakers at every level of the process should be free from conflicts of interest. This is a fundamental element of accountability. Just as public servants are expected to be neutral, dispassionate, and fair in their judgments, so too must rulemakers in private groups. If conflicts are inherent in the structure of the organization, then either the structure should be changed or a mechanism to remove any conflicts must be devised. Individuals with conflicts of interest should be required to recuse themselves from both discussion and decisionmaking. For example, bankers who stand to benefit from Libor rates (overnight, interbank lending rates) should not be permitted to set them because self-dealing under such circumstances can and does occur.[28]

The second minimum consideration involves the nature of the decisions themselves and touches on inclusion. Whenever decisions incorporate value choices, they must be guided by public welfare rather than industry preference if the two conflict.[29] Third, private governance should be more transparent, open to the press and to the public. The bright light of publicity helps keep everyone honest. And open standards, freely available to the public, are preferable to closed ones that are proprietary and must be purchased.

How to ensure that these three expectations are met is a difficult problem. Government has a large role to play, but so do the groups' norms. The next three chapters explore how these groups operate in three fields of endeavor—finance, food safety, and the learned professions—and apply some reasonable standards to which they should be held. What is the relationship between private policymaking groups, governments, and the public? Are the public's concerns recognized, represented, and incorporated in their decisions? If so, how? Are markets enhanced or distorted to benefit those who are making the policy? Are conflicts of interest avoided? Is rulemaking transparent? Are records kept, and are they open to the public? Are known standard operating procedures in place and followed systematically? In what way and to whom are groups held accountable? In short, to what degree is private governance subject to even minimal standards of democratic accountability?

Four

PRIVATE GOVERNANCE IN FINANCE

Private governance permeates financial activities in both the United States and other nations. Internationally, independent mechanisms help close the global governance gap. Here and abroad, the major players in finance are politically potent and have historically been able to promote private over public governance.

Today it is easier to identify government-only regulators than to specify the many, overlapping, and hybrid forms of financial governance. A glance through the *Wall Street Journal* or the *Financial Times* illustrates this point; both use the word "regulators" without saying *which* regulators. Because of the volume and diversity of governing forces shaping investments, securities, banking, accounting, and the stock markets—forces that are often intermingled and working together—distinguishing public from private governance is just about impossible.

To take a few examples at the national level, the Financial Accounting Standards Board (FASB) is a private, nonprofit group overseen by its parent nonprofit group, the Financial Accounting Foundation (FAF), which selects FASB's board members.[1] FASB is recognized legally as an independent organization that sets accounting standards for U.S. corporations, both for-profit and not-for-profit.[2] The governmental Securities and Exchange Commission (SEC) relies on FASB's rules, as does the private, self-regulatory Financial Industry Regulating Authority (FINRA), a creature of the New York Stock Exchange[3] and the now-defunct National Association of Securities Dealers (NASD).[4] As FINRA states on its website, "Federal law gives FINRA the authority to discipline securities firms and individuals in the securities industry who violate the rules."[5] Stated simply, the government hands over its regulatory authority to a private sector entity.

The private association of accountants, the American Institute of Certified Public Accountants (AICPA), also helps set accounting rules, though its role in this regard was diminished in 1973 when FASB was established, and again in 2002.[6] In response to accounting scandals at major corporations such as Enron, Tyco, and WorldCom, in 2002 Congress passed the Sarbanes-Oxley Act, which overhauled standard-setting and established yet another private sector nonprofit corporation, the Public Company Accounting Oversight Board (PCAOB), whose audit rules must be approved by the SEC. Under the new law, auditors of public companies are subject to the authority of rules set by the PCAOB. Still, CPAs continue to be a fundamental building block of the system of financial regulation, as does the AICPA, their self-regulatory organization. (See box 4-1 on the performance of major accounting firms and their CPAs.)

At the state level, state securities administrators oversee investment activities in their jurisdictions. However, typical of virtually all U.S. professions, these officials have united across jurisdictions, in this case to form the North American State Securities Administrators Association (NASAA), a private organization of state public authorities. NASAA creates the FINRA-administered tests that individuals must pass to become state-licensed securities dealers, broker-dealers, and representatives.[7] (Similarly, the AICPA creates and administers the Uniform CPA Examination that all states require for a CPA license.)

BOX 4-1. *How Well Have the Major Accounting*
Firms Performed?

The record of major accounting firms over the past three decades has been less than stellar from a public interest standpoint. These firms accorded clean or unqualified audits—meaning that the financial statements of an audited company accurately report the true condition of its finances and that its financial situation is solid—to corporations that later were found to be anything but sound. These egregious inaccuracies in part led to substantial losses for investors and in some cases for uninvolved bystanders and taxpayers. That fallout included the Latin American debt crisis and the savings and loan debacle of the 1980s; accounting manipulations that contributed to huge losses for investors in Waste Management Corp. (after massive fraud between 1992 and 1997 was revealed), among others, the dot.com collapse of the late 1990s and early 2000s; and most recently, the global financial crisis of 2007–08.[a]

Consider just one example of the irregularities. Auditors did not challenge companies for using improper accounting methods to exaggerate profits or hide losses. The practice, known as "managed earnings," contributed to the two largest corporate bankruptcies in the country's history up to their time, Enron in 2001 and WorldCom in 2002, in which investors, employees, and retirees suffered enormous losses and, in many cases, financial ruin.

Although there were numerous culprits, including public institutions such as the Fed and the SEC, accounting firms' advisory services were partly responsible for the dodgy investment vehicles that set the stage for the global financial crisis, which has been compared to the Great Depression. Specifically, major accounting firms failed to signal significant accounting deficiencies in the large investment banks. Lehman Brothers, the huge financial institution that was the first domino to fall, consistently received a clean bill of health from its

(continued)

"independent" auditor, Ernst and Young, even though Lehman cooked the books in an apparent attempt to hide tens of billions of dollars in liabilities. Lehman's bankruptcy in September 2008, according to the web source Investopedia, "was a seminal event that greatly intensified the 2008 crisis and contributed to the erosion of close to $10 trillion in market capitalization [the total value of companies' outstanding shares] from global equity markets in October 2008, the biggest monthly decline on record at the time."[b]

The sloppiness and, in some cases, misfeasance continue. Despite reforms enacted after the catastrophes mentioned above, the government watchdog PCAOB found in 2013 that the major accounting firms did not adhere to proper procedures almost half of the time and that the failures stemmed from inadequate justification for their statements or "opinions" about a company's financial soundness. That is, they were careless at best, misleading at worst.[c]

The accounting industry has fought such apparently reasonable reforms as regularly rotating auditors, restricting conflicts of interest created by the auditing firms' business models, and requiring the senior partner to sign the results of an accounting engagement—all aimed at improving the functioning, reliability, and accountability of the auditing process. After Britain started requiring audit partners to be identified in 2009, auditors issued more qualified opinions.[d] In the response of all the firms implicated in the crisis, the theme is one of constant pushback against governmental efforts to ensure their accountability and against the firms' obligations to the public.

Article II of the Principles of Professional Conduct, Code of Professional Conduct (AICPA), summarizes CPAs' obligations to the public: "Members should accept the obligation to act in a way that will serve the public interest, honor the public trust, and demonstrate commitment to professionalism."

The AICPA's requirement that its members "serve the public interest [and] honor the public trust" seems to be outweighed by harder realities. If a CPA works for one of the big four accounting firms in particular, a multiple-principals problem can arise, as a continuation of the statement above acknowledges: "[M]embers may encounter conflicting pressures from among each of those groups [that the accountants serve]. In resolving those conflicts, members should act with integrity, guided by the precept that when members fulfill their responsibility to the public, clients' and employers' interests are best served."

The CPA's obligations to the accounting profession, one principal, can conflict with the CPA's desire to serve her client-conscious employer, another principal. One example arises in a report by the International Consortium of Investigative Journalists, which asserts that 340 "companies have channeled hundreds of billions of dollars through Luxembourg and saved billions of dollars" in taxes they would otherwise owe various governments. The article cites PricewaterhouseCoopers as having helped multinational companies obtain at least 548 tax rulings in Luxembourg from 2002 to 2010. These legal but secret deals feature complex financial structures designed to create drastic tax reductions. The rulings provide written assurance that companies' tax saving plans will be viewed favorably by Luxembourg authorities.[c] However much these practices serve profit-seeking clients, they arguably breach the accountants' code of conduct, the public trust, and the public interest.

a. According to a report from the Federal Reserve, "by 1982, the nine largest US money-center banks held Latin American debt amounting to 176 percent of their capital; their total LDC debt was nearly 290 percent of capital." Joycelyn Sims and Jessie Romero, "Latin American Debt Crisis of the 1980s: A Detailed Essay on an Important Event in the History of the Federal Reserve" (Federal Reserve System of the United States, November 22, 2013) (www.federalreservehistory.org/Events/Detail View/46).

b. "Case Study: The Collapse of Lehman Brothers" (www.investopedia .com/articles/economics/09/lehman-brothers-collapse.asp). Technically, Bear Stearns might be named the first fatality of the crisis, but it tends to be treated by observers as the rumbling before the earthquake.

(continued)

c. See Floyd Norris, "Accounting World, Still Resisting Sunlight," *New York Times*, October, 25, 2013.

d. See Joseph V. Carcello and Chan Li, "Costs and Benefits of Requiring an Engagement Partner Signature: Recent Experience in the United Kingdom," *Accounting Review* 8, no. 5 (September–October 2013): 1511–46.

e. "Big 4 Audit Firms Play Big Role in Offshore Murk," November 5, 2014 (www.icij.org/project/luxembourg-leaks/big-4-audit-firms-play-big-role -offshore-murk).

Also at the state local levels is FASB's counterpart for public sector accounting standards, the independent Governmental Accounting Standards Board (GASB), which sets the accounting rules that state and local governments must follow and thus directly regulates governmental entities.[8] Like FASB, GASB derives its authority from the private FAF, which chooses its board members and oversees its operations. In many cases, state law mandates adherence to GASB standards. But as a practical matter, any public entity that wishes to float bonds in the securities market to raise money for infrastructure and other projects must receive a rating from one of the handful of private credit-rating corporations—and only public authorities that follow GASB rules can receive a passing rating.[9] GASB has much to account for. To give only one example, states and localities, following GASB's weak rules, now have an estimated total of $1 trillion in unfunded pension liabilities, potentially leaving either taxpayers in the future to make up the difference or pensioners with less to live on than promised.[10] Figure 4-1 shows the groups that compose the private accounting regime.

The following extended examples illustrate several points. First, public and private sector bodies are deeply intertwined in creating and enforcing accounting, investment, and other financial rules and practices.

Second, private self-regulatory organizations (SROs) help create public policy and enforce rules for various industries and professions.

FIGURE 4-1. *Network of Private Governance in Accounting*

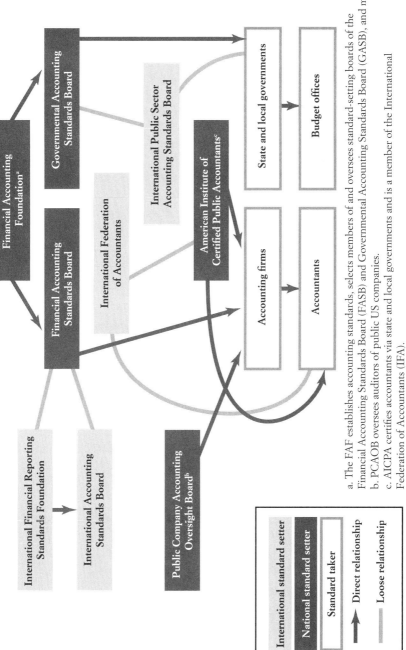

a. The FAF establishes accounting standards, selects members of and oversees standard-setting boards of the Financial Accounting Standards Board (FASB) and Governmental Accounting Standards Board (GASB), and more.

b. PCAOB oversees auditors of public US companies.

c. AICPA certifies accountants via state and local governments and is a member of the International Federation of Accountants (IFA).

Some of these private groups share authority with a governmental body; others constitute the primary regulatory body in an area where there is little government oversight. SROs are recognized in a law that mandates certain activities but they operate independently. For example, the Securities Investor Protection Corporation (SIPC) was created by the Securities Investor Protection Act of 1970 to insure investors who are defrauded by a broker. The SIPC is a nonprofit membership organization without formal regulatory authority, yet the legislation mandates that most U.S. broker-dealers join SIPC and pay dues to support its activities.[11] Another example of an SRO is the PCAOB, a private governance organization. This hybrid body must submit its rules

---

BOX 4-2. *The PCAOB's Standard-Setting Process: Combining Private Governance and Government*

The Sarbanes-Oxley Act of 2002 directed the Public Company Accounting Oversight Board to establish auditing and related professional practice standards for registered public accounting firms to follow in preparing and issuing audit reports. In July 2010, the Dodd-Frank Wall Street Reform and Consumer Protection Act amended the Sarbanes-Oxley Act and authorized the PCAOB to establish auditing and related professional practice standards for audits of the financial statements and selected practices and procedures of broker-dealers. The Board's Office of the Chief Auditor develops these standards.

The Board has sought to allow a wide variety of stakeholders—including investors, auditors, preparers of financial statements, and other standard-setters and regulators—to provide input on standards as they are developed.

The Board's Standing Advisory Group also weighs in on the standard-setting agenda and related matters. Additionally, the Board

to a governmental body, the SEC, for approval. Yet it is incorporated as a private entity. (See box 4-2 for a description of its rulemaking process.) Is the PCAOB public or private?[12]

Third, organizations such as the states' NASAA are technically and legally private and yet—like a number of private governance organizations—are composed exclusively of government administrators. Is NASAA public or private?

Globally, the boundary between public and private is further blurred. A host of quasi-private groups influence the activities of financial regulators. The relatively obscure but highly influential Bank for International Settlements (BIS) in Basel, Switzerland, coordinates

may use public roundtables, focus groups, and task forces to discuss certain standard-setting topics. The Board also takes into account observations from its inspections of registered public accounting firm audits and other oversight activities.

Depending on the nature of the project, the Board may issue a concept release to solicit public comment before issuing a proposed standard. Typically, after the Board reviews any feedback, it proceeds to develop a draft standard. After issuing the proposed standard and related release for public comment, the Board considers the comments and determines whether to adopt the proposed standard as final or re-propose the standard for additional public comment. Once the standard has been adopted, the Board then submits it to the Securities and Exchange Commission for approval.

The SEC solicits public comment on the Board's standard and decides whether to approve it. A PCAOB standard does not become effective unless and until it is approved by the SEC.

Source: From Public Company Accounting Oversight Board, http:// pcaobus.org/Standards/Pages/StandardSettingProcess.aspx.

central banks, national banks that manage a country's currency and interest rates in their quest for monetary and financial stability, and serves as a bank for central banks.[13] According to one extensive account, the BIS in effect operates as an exclusive club. Only central bankers of the most prosperous countries participate at the highest level of this largely opaque organization.[14] Or take the example of the previously mentioned "private" International Organization of Securities Commissions (IOSCO), established in 1983. It is "the acknowledged international body that brings together the world's securities regulators and is recognized as the global standard setter for the securities sector."[15]

Further, there is the Financial Stability Board (FSB), hosted at the BIS in Basel. A private, independent body, the FSB exists "to coordinate at the international level the work of national financial authorities and international standard setting bodies and to develop and promote the implementation of effective regulatory, supervisory and other financial sector policies." Its members are national officials responsible for financial stability in "significant international financial centers, international financial institutions, sector-specific international groupings of regulators and supervisors, and committees of central bank experts."[16] This private regulator, composed of elite central bankers, determines the capital standards that systemically important banks— so-called too-big-to-fail institutions—must meet, to protect their own interests and coordinate policy with other countries. This work is coordinated with the BIS's Basel Committee on Banking Supervision. The intent is to ensure that no bank creates a global financial panic, as happened in 2007–08, because it has insufficient resources to meet its obligations to its creditors. Minimum capital requirements are meant to preclude the need for the public to bail out a failing institution.[17]

Other such global organizations are the International Financial Reporting Standards Foundation and its subsidiary, the International Accounting Standards Board; the International Federation of Accountants and its affiliate, the International Public Sector Accounting

Board; and the International Association of Insurance Supervisors.[18] In closing the global governance gap, these private groups can lose sight of exactly whom or what they represent. The lengthy chain of representation from sovereign citizens to these groups' decisions is both tenuous and opaque. To the degree that regulatory changes agreed to at the global level must be publicized, scrutinized, and formally approved by representative institutions back home, some accountability is ensured. However, to the degree that "national representatives" participating in private global rulemaking groups can act unilaterally and in private, little accountability is likely. Just as important, the concerns of less-powerful, less-developed countries are probably underrepresented, if represented at all, in these global rulemaking platforms.

WHEN PRIVATE GOVERNANCE IS USED—AND WHEN IT IS CURTAILED

Much of the history of financial regulation can be seen through two opposing lenses. First is the sector's strong preference for self-regulation whenever possible and, failing that, considerable distance between citizens and decisionmakers. Second, after serious scandal or apparently irresponsible behavior in the private sector, government oversight is created or heightened.

That government functions best when it governs least, to paraphrase Thomas Jefferson, has served as a guiding principle over much of U.S. history. The Founders' fear of populism, fickle publics, ignorance, and mob rule is part of the DNA of American government.[19] The authors of the Constitution were especially fearful that people with fewer resources, the majority, would want to take money through legislative means from the affluent, so the Constitution was structured to limit majority rule. In the twentieth century, this lack of trust in "the people" led to distancing the public from decisionmaking on questions such as accounting rules, securities regulation, and target interest rates and employment levels.[20]

The first lens provides a clear view of the U.S. Federal Reserve System (the Fed), led by a presidentially appointed and congressionally approved chairman of the Federal Reserve Board of Governors. The Fed, primarily through its Federal Open Market Committee, effectively sets interest rates and works to control inflation and maximize employment; it also provides liquidity to the banking system and performs many other functions to stabilize banking and credit. In the wake of the global financial crisis, it has become the most important regulator of the banking industry.[21] Despite its enormous power, the Fed is and has described itself as "independent," though that word seems to have disappeared from its website.[22] Although the fixed-term chairman must testify before Congress when asked and periodically meets with the president, he or she is not legally compelled to follow congressional or presidential instruction. The rules the Fed sets for U.S. banks are not subject to presidential or congressional review. Nor are the presidents of the twelve regional member banks selected in a public process or approved by Congress, though the seven-member Board of Governors (five of whose members are drawn from among the member-bank presidents) are nominated by the president and confirmed by the Senate.[23] Moreover, Congress's "power of the purse"—that is, its ability to withhold funds when an agency does not perform according to its wishes—is irrelevant, because the Fed has its own sources of funds from member banks and the ability to create money. The Fed, in other words, is a governmental institution far removed from popular control. While technically a hybrid, fourth-arena institution, in many ways the Fed acts like a private governance or fifth-arena organization, a fact that underscores the murky boundary between public and private in current parlance.

One factor that has strengthened the argument for self-regulation in finance is the growing complexity of financial products and services (such as derivatives, leveraging techniques, subprime loans, high-frequency trading, and esoteric structured securities) and the necessity for high-level expertise to regulate them. Even among financial experts, knowledge is limited to specialized areas, with the result that understanding the consequences of even one policy, much less regulating the overall financial system, is extremely difficult. This complexity provides cover for adverse financial news and obscures the answers to Mashaw's accountability questions: accountability to whom, by whom, about what, through what processes, by what standards, and with what effect?[24]

The second lens illuminates an opposite movement toward increased public oversight via congressionally mandated reforms arising from industry misdeeds and inadequate "self-regulation." More governmental regulation, scrutiny, and new oversight agencies were all part of Congress's response to accounting scandals early in this century and the global financial crisis. By 2010, when Dodd-Frank was enacted, a common understanding of the meltdown had developed, and lax private and public regulation was seen as a major cause.[25] Fraud, deceit, collusion, lack of vigilance, and conflicts of interest within the very groups that should have been regulating their industries and providing accurate information to investors called for strengthening government oversight and conceding some private authority to public institutions. A good example of the stripping of private authority is found in the reduction of the AICPA's formal power in 2002. Crisis-response tends to follow that pattern, but it may also lead to the creation by government of additional private watchdogs, such as the PCAOB that same year and the Consumer Financial Protection Bureau in 2010.

In summary, financial regulation might be properly understood as standing as far as possible from direct popular control, a disposition that can be forfeited when the regulatory system fails to protect the public.

SELF-REGULATORY ORGANIZATIONS: A DOMINANT FORM IN FINANCE

Among the organizational forms that private governing institutions take, one in particular, the self-regulatory organization (SRO), is prominent in financial regulation. SROs are expected to make and enforce their own rules and enforce federal securities law—in both cases subject to approval by the SEC—and provide the backbone of U.S. securities regulation.[26] They include national security (stock) exchanges that operate in the United States and elsewhere, such as Intercontinental Exchange (ICE)'s New York Stock Exchange and NASDAQ; securities futures exchanges such as the Chicago Mercantile Exchange; registered securities clearinghouses that reconcile the trades made on the exchanges; the Securities Investor Protection Corporation (SIPC); and the National Futures Association (NFA), among others. To illustrate, we describe two of them in more detail here: the Financial Industry Regulatory Authority (FINRA) and the Municipal Securities Rulemaking Board (MSRB).[27]

The distinction between self-regulatory and entirely self-governing entities is significant. First, SROs are recognized by statute, authorized to enforce laws, and operate to a degree under the supervision of the SEC. Submitting to their authority is mandatory for specified groups and individuals. The degree to which SROs, as agents of the U.S. government, are subject to the same constitutional requirements, such as due process, as federal agencies that perform comparable rulemaking and enforcement duties with the force of law is unresolved by the courts. From a democratic standpoint, this unsettled status detracts from the merits of SROs, as does the lack of public access to their proceedings. Private organizations are not covered under the Freedom of Information Act, nor must they, in making rules, follow the Administrative Procedure Act, which spells out the public participation and procedural requirements of government agencies. These limitations impair the ability of the financial press to cover and interpret the activities of these groups and of the public to be cognizant of their activities, much less influence them.

COMMONALITIES AMONG SROS

SROs, however varied, share certain characteristics beyond wielding formal legal authority. They are not identified as governmental, and they typically describe themselves as "independent." All are self-funded and rely on no public money, one putative advantage of assigning governmental functions to SROs. Revenues of independent organizations regulating finance derive mostly from fees that operate as taxes on the industry's most direct participants. For example, the MSRB collects fees from dealers in municipal securities.[28] In addition, the MSRB sells subscriptions to its proprietary data. The mission and rulemaking process of the MSRB are described in box 4-3 in an excerpt from its rulebook.

Another commonality among SROs is their ability to set employee compensation far higher than that of similarly qualified and situated public servants. For instance, SEC chair Mary Jo White earned $165,300 (not including fringe benefits) in 2014, a mere 6 percent of the $2.624 million paid to FINRA president and CEO Richard Ketchum, according to FINRA's 2013 annual report.[29] Other SEC staff professionals, too, are much more poorly paid than their private sector counterparts. This difference in remuneration, along with such factors as hiring and budget limits, severely limits the SEC's effectiveness. A metaphorical revolving door creates significant conflicts of interest for SEC personnel who may wish to be employed in the future by firms they are regulating and who, despite being public servants, may cater to those firms.[30]

BOX 4-3. *What the Municipal Securities*
Rulemaking Board Does

The mission of the Municipal Securities Rulemaking Board (MSRB) is to protect investors, state and local governments and other municipal entities, and the public interest by promoting a fair and efficient municipal securities market. The MSRB fulfills this mission by regulating the municipal securities firms, banks and municipal advisors that engage in municipal securities and advisory activities. To further protect market participants, the MSRB provides market transparency through its Electronic Municipal Market Access (EMMA®) website, the official repository for information on all municipal bonds. The MSRB also serves as an objective resource on the municipal market, conducts extensive education and outreach to market stakeholders, and provides market leadership on key issues. The MSRB is a Congressionally-chartered, *self-regulatory organization* governed by a 21-member board of directors that *has a majority of public members,* in addition to representatives of regulated entities. The MSRB is subject to oversight by the Securities and Exchange Commission.

MSRB's majority-public board of directors is composed of 21 members, including representatives of regulated entities, investors, municipal entities and other members of the public. The Board of Directors meets throughout the year to make policy decisions, authorize rulemaking, enhance information systems and review developments in the municipal market. A professional staff in Alexandria, Virginia manages the MSRB's day-to-day operations.

Rulemaking Process

The Securities Exchange Act sets forth certain areas in which the MSRB is directed to conduct rulemaking, including rules to prevent fraudulent and manipulative acts and practices, to promote just and equitable principles of trade and to serve various other specific purposes described in the Act. In order to provide the maximum opportunity for industry participation, the MSRB generally publishes rule-making proposals as requests for comment and provides for public comment periods.

In the earliest stages of rulemaking, the MSRB may issue a concept proposal. A concept proposal assists the Board in assessing whether to undertake rulemaking with regard to a particular matter. A concept proposal does not represent a formal rulemaking proposal by the Board and its issuance does not obligate the Board to move forward with a proposal. Substantive comments on rule proposals received as a result of these procedures continue to influence the MSRB's deliberations. Upon adoption by the MSRB in final form, rule proposals are filed with the SEC. In its rule filings, the MSRB is required to address the terms and purpose of the proposed rules, the statutory basis for their adoption, an analysis of the comments received and the statutory justification for any anticipated burden on competition the rule proposals might impose. The Securities Exchange Act requires the SEC to publish the MSRB's rule proposals in the Federal Register for public comment. MSRB rules only become effective upon approval by the SEC or, in very limited circumstances provided under the Securities Exchange Act, immediately upon filing with the SEC. Upon becoming effective, *MSRB rules have the force and effect of federal law.*

The *MSRB's rules are enforced by* the Financial Industry Regulatory Authority (FINRA) for securities firms, by bank regulatory agencies (the Board of Governors of the Federal Reserve System, the Office of the Comptroller of the Currency and the Federal Deposit Insurance Corporation) for banks, and by the SEC for municipal advisors and all securities firms and banks. An important aspect of its rulemaking activities involves the ongoing interpretation of its rules. This is done by means of interpretive letters and notices.

Source: MSRB Rules (www.msrb.org/Rules-and-Interpretations/MSRB -Rules.aspx), emphasis added. The MSRB's rulemaking process is similar to that of other SROs.

SELF-GOVERNING ORGANIZATIONS

Not-for-profit self-governing organizations (SGOs) have even more freedom than SROs. SGOs determine their own rules, and when those rules substantially affect a public broader than their members or stockholders, they function as private governance organizations. Unlike SROs, they are not invested with formal governmental authority. If they are membership organizations, belonging to them is voluntary but typically restricted by the groups' bylaws. Their form varies, though usually these groups are not-for-profit associations of people or firms or are associations of associations. Their enforcement powers are limited, but civil courts may force compliance through their rulings. Because SGOs are private, they are not obliged to reveal what they do, how they operate, who their members are, or what decisions they make. For the most part, they are accountable only to themselves.

Only some of the activities of SGOs qualify as private governance in the sense of making policy that substantially affects a larger public. Some examples of SGOs are the Securities Industry and Financial Markets Association, the Investment Company Institute, the American Bankers Association, and the American Institute of Certified Public Accountants. Their primary missions are advocacy and related activities, and their rules apply only to their members; to repeat, however, industry rules and standards can bleed beyond the organizations making them, qualifying them as private governance groups, as in the case of the AICPA. Besides SROs and SGOs, for-profit corporations, such as those that rate securities, can also engage in private governance, as discussed later in this chapter. Box 4-4 provides a classification of the types of private governance groups in finance according to their relationship with government.

Policymaking SROs and SGOs both would likely point out not only that their work is "free" to the government but also that their expertise in developing workable and efficient regulations is a valuable public good. Websites of many of these organizations assert that they

---

BOX 4-4. *Classification of Private Governance Organizations in Finance According to Their Relationship with Government*

Tax-Exempt Associations and Boards

Self-regulatory organizations are self-governing, independent organizations recognized by statute and authorized to govern in specified areas. Some examples are FINRA, stock exchanges, MSRB, FASB, and PCAOB. Some, such as FINRA, are legally authorized to enforce their own rules, refer violations to the SEC and other agencies, and uphold specific U.S. laws.

Self-governing organizations (SGOs) are independent organizations composed of individual and/or organizational members representing a profession or industry. Only some SGOs operate as independent private governance organizations making public policy, and this role is typically not primary. National SGOs in finance are largely engaged in member representation with governmental bodies. If an SGO creates industry standards or "best practices," the judiciary may rely on them for resolving cases. An example of a private governance organization in the form of an SGO is the AICPA in its certification of practitioners and its enforcement of professional ethical standards.

For-Profit Corporations

Private firms' purpose is to maximize their profits. When their determinations significantly affect the larger public, they function as private governance organizations. NRSROs (nationally recognized statistical rating organizations), specifically the "big three" credit-rating organizations, Standard & Poor's, Fitch, and Moody's are the best examples in the area of finance. Their ratings are relied upon by governments, firms, and investors for a variety of purposes.

serve the public and, in many cases, that protecting the public and investors is their primary mission. They are less likely to highlight the conflicts of interest that can arise when an industry regulates itself to a large extent. The paltry enforcement efforts, for example, leading up to the financial crisis of 2007–08 were typical not only of government agencies (the SEC, the Federal Deposit Insurance Corporation [FDIC], the Treasury, the Commodities Futures Trading Commission and the Federal Reserve's Board of Governors) but also of SROs such as FINRA.[31] All of them seemed to have been slumbering since at least 2005 and largely out of touch with the financial depredations of Wall Street.[32] Needless to say, neither investors nor the wider public was protected sufficiently during this period, although large securities firms on the whole were.[33]

FINANCIAL INDUSTRY REGULATORY AUTHORITY (FINRA): THE BEHEMOTH OF SROS

In the wake of the Great Depression and the 1930s New Deal reforms designed to prevent future financial meltdowns, Congress agreed to involve industry participants in its regulation of securities trading. The organization recruited to create and enforce rules for securities dealers—under the supervision of a newly created SEC—was the National Association of Securities Dealers (NASD), an existing private membership organization. Professionals who traded for the public fell within the aegis of the NASD. At the same time, the stock exchanges had their own rules for themselves and their members. The oldest and largest of these trading platforms, the New York Stock Exchange with its subsidiaries and partners, eventually created a separate SRO, NYSE Regulation, Inc., to perform these functions with a putative goal of protecting investors. In 2007 the SEC approved a consolidation of the regulatory functions of the NASD and NYSE Regulation, and the result was FINRA, Inc.[34]

Understanding the size and importance of FINRA in the securities industry requires only a look at a recent annual report. FINRA is exceptionally well endowed, with assets in 2013 totaling $2.257 billion. That year, it reported that it had meted out 1,535 disciplinary actions and $60 million in fines, expelled twenty-five firms from the industry and suspended the activities of thirty-eight others, barred 429 individuals from trading, suspended 670 brokers from associating with FINRA-regulated firms, ordered restitution to fraud victims ($32 million in 2014), and referred 660 fraud and insider-trading cases to the SEC and other agencies for possible prosecution. These activities capture only a part of FINRA's raison d'être. FINRA explains that it "touches virtually every aspect of the securities business—from registering and educating all industry participants to examining securities firms, writing rules, enforcing those rules and the federal securities laws, informing and educating the investing public, providing trade reporting and other industry utilities, and administering the largest dispute resolution forum for investors and firms." FINRA states that it is dedicated to "investor protection" and "market integrity."[35]

To say that FINRA's impact on the public (their resources, their financial health, and the fiscal well-being of the country, even the world) is substantial is a vast understatement. How well does FINRA meet the criteria of democratic legitimacy: accountability, transparency, and inclusiveness? Are conflicts of interest avoided? Are FINRA activities market-enhancing? Answering these questions requires a closer examination of the FINRA's rulemaking process.

JURISDICTION, RULEMAKING, AND PUBLIC REPRESENTATION

FINRA establishes and enforces the rules for the registered participants in the securities industry: what they can and cannot do, their professional obligations, the representations they can make to clients, and the information they must disclose when selling products. But its jurisdiction over trading is not unlimited. For instance, before the Great Recession it had not paid much attention to trading in "dark pools" of capital or private trading of investment instruments—secret trading not open to the general public.[36] Regulation here is still lacking, as it is in derivatives trading.[37]

The first important takeaway is that a multitude of SROs regulate the securities industry; although FINRA is by far the largest and arguably the most important of them, much lies outside its purview. The

---

BOX 4-5. *FINRA'S Rulemaking Process in Brief*

Seventeen FINRA advisory committees, each with staff liaisons, help guide rulemaking from agenda setting to the writing of a regulation. Suggestions for an amendment or a new standard are not limited to the advisory committees but may also derive from the large professional staff, the board of directors, the SEC, or other interested parties both inside and beyond FINRA. Putting a possible change on the radar of the FINRA rulemakers is, in other words, expert driven, industry driven, and to a lesser and largely indirect degree, motivated by investor concerns. The fact that FINRA is considering a rule is not publicly announced at this early stage. Hence FINRA sets the agenda with all of the power that offers and does so in private.

After a proposed rule is discussed and developed within FINRA, the board of directors must agree that the rule is appropriate and should move forward. Minutes of the board and its committees are not made public. Hence the press is not privy to and has little opportunity to report on the work and thinking of the board, even though the work of the board is arguably the public's business.

FINRA may, upon the board's approval, issue a Regulatory Notice asking for public comment on a new regulation rule or amendment. This stage of soliciting broader opinion is not mandatory, however.

second is that FINRA's rulemaking process, described in box 4-5, is typical of SROs under the general supervision of the SEC, though FINRA is exceptionally well staffed and well endowed.

Over time, FINRA's board membership has come to include a broader range of people and is thus presumably less parochial in its concerns and more conscious of conflicts of interest. The board consists of twenty-two members or "governors," including FINRA's CEO; eleven public governors; and ten industry governors. Seven of these are elected by member firms; the remaining fifteen are nominated by

If a Regulatory Notice is issued, all comments received are to be promptly posted on FINRA's website and become part of the official record. Unlike federal rulemaking procedure under the Administrative Procedure Act, FINRA is under no obligation to address objections to the proffered rule. With the board's concurrence the proposal may be altered at this point, approved in its original form, or withdrawn.

If FINRA decides to move forward with the proposal, as amended, it is then filed with the SEC, whose staff reviews its consistency with the 1934 Securities Exchange Act, as amended. This statute provides the legal basis for FINRA's regulatory and enforcement work. If the staff does not request further alterations, under most circumstances the SEC publishes the rule for twenty-one days in the Federal Register, seeking comment. Upon request from the SEC staff, FINRA must respond to any comments and might—or might not—amend the proposed rule. Once the SEC approves the final rule, the new provision is published in the Federal Register and FINRA publishes its own Regulatory Notice.

Source: See http://finra.complinet.com/en/display/display_main.html?rbid =2403&element_id=4840&print=1. For more information on SROs, see www.sec.gov/rules/sro.shtml.

the Nominations Committee and appointed by the board. In other words, the board is largely self-perpetuating, and its composition is tightly controlled. Its three-year terms are staggered and limited to two. The rules thus ensure a "circulation of elites" and representation of different tiers (by size) of the industry. Whom the "public" members represent is difficult to determine. According to the FINRA rules, a public governor "has no material business relationship with a broker or dealer or a self-regulatory organization registered under the Act."[38] Little other guidance is provided. Simply naming a director as "public" does not ensure that the public's interests are adequately represented or even represented at all. Given FINRA's insistence that it exists to protect the investor, the composition of its board of governors gives pause. However, other aspects of the rulemaking process seem to invite more direct investor and public involvement, as box 4-5 shows.

To a degree, FINRA's rulemaking procedure is transparent, allows for public comment, and is accountable to the SEC. However, FINRA is not subject to FOIA, and the public is not privy to its internal discussions. Further, to say that FINRA's rulemaking is subject to SEC oversight does not mean that it has a direct connection with the public. In the context of democratic legitimacy, arguing that most of the public knows little about securities is an inadequate defense of a private group's making and enforcing public policy. The public knows little about many issues but in a democracy retains the right to representation and redress. More attention might be paid to the underlying concerns of the public if it were more fully informed and represented in the policymaking process. That the SEC must approve FINRA's rules provides more connection to the public than would be the case otherwise. This connection requires vigilance and vigor on the part of the SEC to ensure that the public's interests are served. The SEC's record in this century has been less than stellar in this regard.[39]

Conflicts of interest are built into FINRA's structure in that its board directly represents specific segments of the securities industry.

Before the financial crisis, FINRA arguably caused little discomfort in the industry, perhaps serving as an apologist. Since then, FINRA seems to have taken its obligations to the public more seriously. For example, it has toughened standards applied to brokers who advise investment clients and has also prevented a major brokerage firm from compelling customers to waive their rights to bring class-action suits. As of 2015, it was considering a proposal to require brokers to provide monthly data on their purchases, sales, and related activities to FINRA to help develop an early warning system about possibly abusive practices. Brokerage firms were unhappy about this proposal and waged a vigorous protest, which suggests that, in this case at least, FINRA is not entirely an industry lapdog even if the board's composition is less than salutary from a public policy point of view.[40] At the same time, FINRA has no rule requiring that brokers must place investors' interests first when providing advice.

With regard to its market-enhancing goal, blaming FINRA's lack of regulation for the financial crisis is a stretch. FINRA was only one of many financial regulators either unaware of or unable to attend to the meltdown at its inception. Even if it had been so inclined, it had little ability to puncture the bubble or halt the mispricing of securities composed of risky subprime mortgages and other questionable, sometimes esoteric, collateralized debt obligations, especially since the credit-rating agencies were affirming their high quality.

SROs such as FINRA inevitably have an industry and epistemic bias. Those who pay attention to FINRA's activities are likely to come from the industry itself, and the experts employed by FINRA most likely share a common intellectual and philosophical point of view. As Timothy J. Fogarty, Mohammed E. A. Hussein, and J. Edward Ketz say about accountants, their professional training and experiences channel their thinking in a particular direction, occluding broader public interests or alternative points of view.[41]

FOR-PROFIT CORPORATIONS: CREDIT RATERS AS
PRIVATE GOVERNANCE INSTITUTIONS

Not all private governance in the financial realm emanates from SROs and SGOs. National and multinational corporations, answerable primarily to their stockholders and intent on maximizing shareholder value above all else, may function as governance institutions. As the next chapter, on food safety and quality, illustrates, corporations frequently take charge of making the rules that are binding on suppliant clients and affect the choices available to the public.

Credit-rating agencies (CRAs) are private firms. They rate or grade securities from AAA (the highest rating, indicating the most secure investment) to D (indicating default).[42] These ratings are intended to assist investors in deciding where to put their money. The ratings also guide financial institutions in lending money for a guaranteed rate of return for a fixed period, after which the nominal value of the loan or bond is redeemed to the investor. The investor should be confident that an investment with a high rating is relatively safe. As the rating declines, the investor assumes more risk that the institution issuing the bond will not be able to meet its obligations to the investor. In return, high risk delivers greater returns in the form of a higher interest rate. A low rating can greatly increase the issuer's cost of raising capital. This description demonstrates the importance of the ratings' accuracy and the raters' objectivity.

In recent years, the most charitable assessment of credit raters' performance is that they have repeatedly been "late to the party." In fact, these companies' optimistic but unreliable ratings contributed to the excessive enthusiasm in the markets during the dot.com bubble and the lead-up to the Great Recession of 2007–09. The global financial crisis lies at the feet of, among others, the credit raters that gave AAA ratings to highly dubious investment vehicles.[43]

Sometimes called "gatekeepers,"[44] CRAs are for-profit corporations that constitute a cartel of firms that have been identified by the federal government, via the SEC, as nationally recognized statistical rating organizations (NRSROs): the long-established "big three"—Standard & Poor's, Moody's Investors Services, and Fitch Ratings—and six others added more recently, partly because of the Credit Rating Agency Reform Act of 2006. The NRSRO concept began in 1975 to provide a short-cut for financial institutions to establish that they met capital requirements set by the SEC.[45] By investing in securities highly rated by an NRSRO, the institutions could circumvent stricter levels of liquidity or cash on hand that might be needed should investors retreat or demand immediate payout. In short, the SEC delegated significant authority and market power to the ratings agencies. Governments, private regulators such as FINRA and FASB, and investors have relied increasingly on CRAs despite their missteps over the past quarter-century.[46] These blunders have continued, even since the global financial crisis.[47]

There are many reasons for those errors, but they seem to arise from the conflicts of interest built into the CRAs' business models, a problem shared by the large auditing firms. (See box 4-1, "How Well Have the Major Accounting Firms Performed?") As for-profit institutions, they must make money for their stockholders, a task at which these privileged corporations excel and a task that creates incentives to rate investments more highly than may be warranted. The conflicts of interest stem from several sources.

First, CRAs are paid directly by the issuers whose bonds they are rating and therefore have good business reasons to please the corporations they are supposed to rate objectively, especially since issuers can shop for higher ratings. If, in initial discussions, S&P seems excessively strict, a company can try its luck at Fitch's.

Second, because CRAs sell other services to issuers, the raters may loosen their ratings to attract extra business. (Though curtailed somewhat by rules implementing Sarbanes-Oxley, auditing firms suffer from a similar conflict.) At the same time, because the approved CRAs constitute an oligopoly, they can charge similar fees and can collude in easing ratings that generate business. For example, the multi-trillion-dollar market in packaged securities known as collateralized debt obligations (CDOs) was made possible by the high ratings assigned by the "big three" CRAs to suspect bundles of debts such as subprime mortgages.[48] To add to the questionable practices, Frank Partnoy points out that Fitch has alleged that S&P and Moody's engaged in "notching," or lowering ratings unless "a substantial portion of the assets in the pool are also rated by them."[49]

Third, CRAs brashly provide unsolicited ratings in an apparent effort to generate more business from issuers. When, for example, the Jefferson County, Colorado, school district decided to use S&P and Fitch, rather than Moody's, for a new bond issue in 1993, Moody's soon voluntarily issued its own "negative outlook" on the bonds, a pointed object lesson for other municipalities in the market for a ratings service. As investors dropped out, the county had to cancel the issue, reprice the bonds, and pay a higher interest rate, at a reported increased cost to the district of $769,000, as Partnoy explains.[50] When the district sued, Moody's asserted that its opinion constituted constitutionally protected speech and won. This legal immunity to both civil and criminal liability is one of the several ways in which CRAs differ from other gatekeepers and protects CRAs from liability for their misappraisals.

The size of CRAs' profits is another way they differ. Once the SEC created the NRSRO concept in the 1970s, the source of credit raters' revenues shifted gradually from subscriptions paid by investors to fees paid by issuers, creating the fundamental conflict of interest on which CRAs rest. As government regulations increasingly came to rely on NRSRO ratings, making them mandatory in many cases, operating margins for Moody's reached an astounding 50 percent, according to Partnoy. The irony, of course, is that the CRAs' function could be performed by a genuinely neutral government agency, as Europe has been considering and has been suggested by two members of Congress, or need not be performed at all, as Partnoy argues, if market-based credit spreads were substituted for credit ratings. Without the NRSRO designation and accompanying government requirements to use them (at all levels of government), the CRA business would likely collapse, along with the conflicts of interest that erode their integrity.[51]

Unfortunately, the SEC has not for the most part implemented reforms enacted by Dodd-Frank, and CRAs have resumed some of their dangerous practices. As *BloombergBusiness* reported in 2013, "Almost six years after the start of the worst financial crisis since the Great Depression, bond issuers are again exploiting credit ratings by seeking firms that will provide high grades on debt backed by assets from auto loans to office buildings considered inappropriate by rivals."[52] As the Council on Foreign Relations reported in 2015, the basic business model of the CRAs remains the same, as does their dominance.[53]

CONCLUSION: CAN THE COURTS PROTECT THE PUBLIC? WHAT ARE SOME ALTERNATIVES?

A comparison between the United States and Europe in their approaches to regulation suggests that the relatively lax regulatory activity in the United States is balanced by its greater tolerance for litigation. Rather than preventing harm, the emphasis is on providing redress through the courts, or after-the-fact accountability. Whether the threat of litigation is adequate to forestall industry mal- and misfeasance is debatable. Many companies' executives knowingly engage in harmful or illegal activities. Instead of changing their behavior, they likely calculate the risk of their misbehavior's being exposed and of being sued, and then incorporate that risk as a cost of doing business. Certainly they do not include the adverse effects of their misbehavior on the economy and the public as part of their calculations. With weak regulators and regulation, their risk of being held accountable is reduced, suggesting that legal redress is a feeble form of restraint on corporations in many cases. Litigation can be very expensive for plaintiffs in both time and money, further restricting the value of private lawsuits as a means of keeping corporations in line. If a company is sued, it can frequently settle out of court in a secret agreement with the plaintiff, with the result that others harmed by the same corporate practice are not compensated. By including everyone injured by a corporate practice, class-action suits should make possible a fairer agreement for all parties concerned, but that route has been curtailed by the Supreme Court, particularly for investors attempting to combine to sue corporations for securities fraud.[54] Thus litigation may restrain the most injurious practices of corporations but is no substitute for strong regulation, especially in the area of finance.

As this book makes clear, robust regulation that is inimical to an industry's interests is unlikely to arise from private governance institutions. In the end, it is government that must protect the public.[55] The question is whether such protection is possible, given the American public's apparent antipathy toward and growing distrust of government, coupled with the entrenchment of private governance. Perhaps the best approach is to pay more attention to private governance institutions; establish best practices that focus on issues of democratic legitimacy; enact more demanding rules, such as those prohibiting conflicts of interest in any private governance institution that enjoys the imprimatur of government; require that any agreements concluded by private groups composed of government officials be subject to public discussion; and find ways around institutions such as CRAs that would render them superfluous. Professional societies also could be much more attentive to their members' potential conflicts of interest and other unethical practices.

Five

PRIVATE GOVERNANCE IN FOOD SAFETY AND QUALITY

Beef, American cheese, sesame seeds, shredded lettuce and onions, sliced pickles, sandwich buns and 72 other lesser known ingredients make up the Big Mac sold in McDonald's restaurants. Are these ingredients safe? Who ensures their safety?

"GMO-free" oil, "naturally grown" grains, "cage-free" chicken, "gluten-free" bread, "fair-trade" coffee. . . . These specially labeled foods are easily found at supermarkets, usually at premium prices. Who sets standards for these products? Who verifies their quality? Who labels them?

As markets for food have proliferated and become more integrated in recent years, two related phenomena dominate the field of food safety and quality: the diminishing ability of the public sector to regulate this global market adequately and an increasing reliance on private groups to get the job done.

Regulating food safety and quality has been government's job since the early twentieth century.[1] The complexity brought on by freer trade, technological innovations, and advances in communications and transportation has required governments to revise, tighten, and increase their food safety rules.[2] Even so, U.S. food regulations promulgated by federal agencies have established only the *minimum standards* that must be met.[3] Meanwhile, inspections have lagged, and it seems impossible for the agencies to keep up, given their statutory and budgetary limits.

At the same time, globalization and trade liberalization have led to a substantial increase in exchange of food products across borders, making the task of ensuring their safety much more troublesome than when health and environmental risks were largely contained within national boundaries. The public's awareness of food hazards has been heightened by well-publicized outbreaks of avian influenza (bird flu), bovine spongiform encephalopathy (mad cow disease), and dioxin in animal feed.[4] Based on its 2011 analysis of food-borne illness, the Centers for Disease Control and Prevention, part of the U.S. Department of Health and Human Services, estimates that approximately one in six Americans fall sick annually—and 3,000 of them die—of food-borne diseases, costing more than $15 billion each year in medical expenses and lost wages.[5] Dealing with threats to the food supply has proven difficult. In addition to national vigilance, minimizing food contamination requires international cooperation. Intergovernmental efforts to address global food safety problems, such as the rules set by the World Trade Organization (Sanitary and Phytosanitary Measures) and the Codex Alimentarius Commission have been insufficient because resources and enforcement mechanisms are lacking and some countries resist the one-size-fits-all approach, creating regulatory gaps among nations.[6]

Nationally, the 2011 Food Safety Modernization Act (FSMA) requires more stringent preventive controls on U.S. farms as well as on imported products. This law mandates that the Food and Drug Administration (FDA) inspect domestic and some foreign food facilities.[7] Its goals are ambitious, but the FSMA is constrained by three factors. First, it focuses narrowly on preventing food-borne illnesses, excluding broader issues such as secondary and longer-term health impacts; second, the statute is not comprehensive, covering only certain areas, certain facilities, certain farms, and certain products; and third, appropriations are too meager to accomplish Congress's apparent intent. Specifically, budget outlays have been inadequate to fund the number of federal employees required to inspect production facilities for food entering the United States. The act directs the FDA to establish an "equivalent level of safety" for imported products as for domestic ones, but the FDA is simply unable to inspect overseas production entirely.[8] Practically, oversight can be achieved only by heavy reliance on private food standards, industry traceability systems, and third-party certification.[9] By default, much regulation—both rulemaking and private inspections—is left to private organizations.

Businesses tend to prefer privately set over government-set standards for various reasons. In some circumstances, businesses are motivated to establish and enforce meaningful standards developed by their own organizations. For example, domestic retailers selling imported food products have strong legal and commercial incentives to ensure the safety and quality of the food they sell. At the least, businesses do not want customers to get sick from their products if illnesses can be traced to their businesses. In addition, in competing with other retailers, they can attract more affluent consumers by selling certified higher-quality food. While the flood of food products entering the United States from all over the world makes quality control by insufficiently staffed governmental agencies impractical, retailers can accomplish what government cannot. They can help create and enforce standards for their suppliers. This power arises because supply chains—from farmer to shipper to manufacturer, or from processor to shipper to retail outlet—have been integrated globally. Hence, one large retailer can single-handedly enforce safety and quality standards by virtue of its size, refusing to buy products that do not meet its standards at any point in the supply chain.

In exercising this power, retailers rely in part on global food safety and quality standards set by private groups such as the American Bakers Association or the Food Marketing Institute (FMI). If suppliers do not accept the retailers' requirements, they stand to lose the sale and market share. This threat is particularly potent in monopsony or oligopsony markets characterized by large retailers, such as Wal-Mart, that absorb a significant proportion of a given market.[10] In fact, the approximately $4 trillion global food market is dominated by a few major food retailers that account for more than 50 percent of the global market share.[11] In the United States, the top four major grocery retailers (Wal-Mart, Kroger, Safeway, and Publix) account for about

FIGURE 5-1. *Retailers' Share of U.S. Grocery Sales, 1992–2012*

Percent of sales

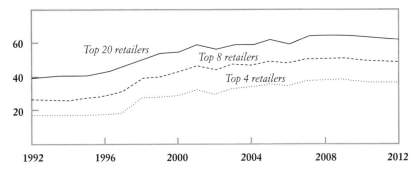

Sources: USDA, Economic Research Service, calculation using data from various sources such as U.S. Census Bureau, Monthly Retail Trade Survey, company annual reports, and other industry sources.

40 percent of the U.S. market share, and the top eight grocery retailers account for about half. These numbers have almost doubled since 1992, as illustrated in figure 5-1.[12]

At the same time, suppliers seeking to enter competitive and demanding U.S. and European markets can use certifications set by major private groups such as the FMI, more stringent than public regulations, to entice retailers to offer their foods to retail customers. Once a supplier follows a set of rules to satisfy a retailer, the supplier is likely to maintain those standards for other perhaps less demanding or less commanding retailers if changing standards would cost more than abiding by them.

ADDITIONAL FORCES SUPPORTING THE GROWTH OF PRIVATE STANDARDS

Several other factors have supported the growing dominance of privately set food safety and quality standards. Technological developments have created ways to increase food production and, arguably, enhance food safety and quality, including fertilizers, additives, preservatives, better storage and delivery methods, and genetically modified organism (GMO) production. Despite their possible benefits, however, some technological developments have also raised consumer concerns about the unknown or lesser-known adverse effects of advanced technologies and chemicals on human health.[13] The inadequacy of visual inspection to determine either immediate safety or long-term impact on health has increased consumer concerns about the composition of their food, including the effect of processing and production methods.[14] Their concerns, and hence some standards, have broadened as shoppers have become more conscious of the possible negative impact of food production not just on their own health but also on animal welfare, the environment, workers' welfare, and global poverty.[15]

One example of growing consumer unease about food technology is the use of GMOs. Since their introduction, controversies have raged over the potential health risks. Public and private GMO-free standards are spreading worldwide, especially in the European Union (EU). In contrast, the U.S. government and food industry assert that GMO technology is based on "sound science" and is safe.[16] In 2013, more than 90 percent of corn, cotton, and soybeans planted in the United States was genetically modified.[17] Responding to consumer preferences, however, many food retailers and manufacturers in Europe and other developed countries have avoided GM crops and ingredients. To meet the demands of more sophisticated and fastidious consumers in countries such as the United States where GMO-altered food is legal, perceived-quality competition among retailers has created a "race to the top," using private standards to certify that food is GMO-free and charge premium prices for that assurance. This effort to certify the composition and production of food extends much further than the use of GMOs. As a result of affluent consumers' concerns, private institutions that certify and enforce exacting standards have become indispensable in contemporary global food markets.[18]

STANDARDS AS A SOURCE OF CONTROL
AND AN EXPRESSION OF NATIONAL VALUES

Individually and collectively, large food retailers and supermarket chains have generated or supported various food safety and quality standards made by private groups. Scholars argue that individual and collective standards are not only serving interests of the major retailers but also transforming the structure of global agricultural and food markets from price-driven into quality-based competition.[19] However, driven mostly by major food retailers, a series of private institutions that set collective food safety and quality standards has been established since the 1990s. Some examples of individually set or single-retailer-based food safety standards include the Carrefour Quality Certification program, Tesco's Nature's Choice, and food standards set by Wal-Mart and Nestlé. To address broader issues, including animal welfare, companies such as McDonald's and Nestlé have been developing and implementing their own standards. The most prominent collective food safety and quality standards created by private (largely retailer-dominated) groups are summarized in table 5-1.

Meeting private standards offers major supermarket chains and large food processors a way to differentiate their products, achieve competitiveness, and dominate the market. The purpose of private standards, however, is not only to identify foods that meet a gold standard of sorts. They also serve to pre-empt more stringent regulatory developments or earn businesses time to prepare for upcoming public regulations, minimize uncertainties arising from countries' national legislation, and reduce liability risks and transaction costs.[20]

Setting private standards also enables large enterprises to achieve greater bargaining power over suppliers and, arguably, to gain greater economic, social, and political control throughout their supply chains.[21] These standards shape in fundamental ways what people eat, how much they pay for food, and how it reaches the dining table. All of this is accomplished mostly without much public knowledge about the

TABLE 5-1. *Prominent Private Standards on Food Safety and Quality*

Private institution and standards, year established, and main region	Activities and importance
British Retail Consortium Global Standards for Food Safety (BRC) 1998, United Kingdom and Scandinavia	Has set more than 250 requirements regarding food safety and quality norms, products and process management, and personal hygiene
International Food Standards (IFS) 2001, Europe	Initiated by German food retailers Collaborations among three retail federations from Germany, France, and Italy
Safe Quality Food (SQF) 1994, United States and global	Originally established by the West Australian Department of Agriculture and bought by the U.S.-based Food Marketing Institute (FMI), a retailer-driven organization, in 2003
Global Food Safety Initiative (GFSI) 2000, global	Initiated by a group of global retailers to support globally recognized food safety standards including BRC, Dutch HACCP, IFS, and SQF[a]
Global Partnership for Good Agricultural Practice (GlobalG.A.P.) 1997, Europe and global	Developed by European retailers GlobalG.A.P. certification requires completion of a checklist of 254 questions Benchmarked existing rules to avoid duplication of standards
Foundation for Food Safety Certification (FSSC) 2004, Europe and global	Developed FSSC 22000 for certification of food manufacturers, based on the ISO 22000 and PAS 220
Global Red Meat Standard (GRMS) 2006, Denmark and global	Specifically developed for red meat industry established by the Danish Agriculture and Food Council

(continued)

TABLE 5-1. *(continued)*

Private institution and standards, year established, and main region	Activities and importance
Marine Stewardship Council (MSC) 1997, Europe and global	A label for sustainable fishery, created by the agreement between Unilever and the World Wildlife Fund
Ethical Trading Initiative (ETI) 1998, U.K.	Established by U.K. trade union representatives from unions such as the Trade Union Congress and NGOs such as Oxfam

a. BRC = British Retail Consortium Global Standards for Food Safety; HACCP = Hazard Analysis Critical Control Points; IFS = International Food Standards; SQF – Safe Quality Food.

Source: Doris Fuchs and others, "Actors in Private Food Governance: The Legitimacy of Retail Standards and Multistakeholder Initiatives with Civil Society Participation," *Agriculture and Human Values* 28 (September 2011); Cecilia Carlsson and Helena Johansson, "Private Standards: Leveling the Playing Field for Global Competition in the Food Supply Chain?," *AgriFood Economic Center Report* (Lund University School of Economics and Management, 2013); and the websites of the organizations (standards) listed.

decisionmaking process. As noted above, although private standards may appear to be voluntary because they are not legally binding, they act as "*de facto mandatory*" rules in current markets.[22] In other words, even without legal punishment for noncompliance, no practical alternative is available for firms and suppliers if they want to enter or remain in important markets.[23]

As shown in table 5-1, most of the predominant collective food standards set by private groups were established in Europe, especially Northern Europe (except the Safe Quality Food [SQF] standards set by the Food Marketing Institute [FMI], a U.S.-based organization).[24] Although less enthusiastic about developing collective standards than their European counterparts, many leading food retailers in the

United States also require their supply-chain partners to follow individual or collective private food standards that they have adopted. Private food standard-setters in the United States include NSF International (formerly National Sanitation Foundation and Davis Fresh), Primus Labs, and the FMI.[25]

While both public and private food standards developed in Europe are concerned with extensive issues, including human health, workers' welfare, animal rights, environmental protection, GMOs, and ethics, most collective food standards developed in the United States focus on narrower issues, such as ensuring sanitary production, shipping and storage, and preventing food-borne illness. A possible reason for this divergence is that U.S. companies prefer to control individual food standards and tend to believe that consumers should have choices that are reflected in prices. The broader collective food standards favored in the Northern European market are facilitated by an industry-wide consensus on these issues in the region.

These cultural and economic differences among nations in food safety and quality standards, both public and private, sometimes cause trade conflicts and coordination problems. One example can be found in the heated debates between the U.S. and European provisions of the Transatlantic Trade and Investment Partnership (proposed in 2013) dealing with such "controversial foods as hormone beef, GMOs, and chlorinated chicken."[26] Practices that are legal or normal in one territory or industry can be illegal or unacceptable in another. The complex global food system constructed by multi-layered rules, including different public regulations in different countries and private standards, including both individually enforced programs and collective programs, have made harmonization among them difficult.

RULEMAKING PROCEDURES: SOME EXAMPLES OF
PRIVATE GOVERNANCE

Standard-setting processes and enforcement mechanisms vary greatly. As mentioned, the broadest distinction is between individually and privately set private food standards. Individual corporations such as Carrefour, Tesco, Wal-Mart, Nestlé, and McDonald's require certain standards in their own supply chains. In contrast, a group of organizations, mostly large retailers, sets collective standards when it serves the group's collective interest. Safe Quality Food (SQF), the Global Food Safety Initiative (GFSI), and GlobalG.A.P. are prominent examples of private governance organizations that set collective standards for the food industry as a whole. Both individually and collectively, standards created by a third-party private organization may be used. Often, certification that standards are being met also is contracted to qualified third-party groups.

Individual Food Standards: McDonald's Quality
and Food Safety Assurance Program

Establishing and managing food safety and quality programs is time-consuming and costly for individual companies, and only multinational, market-dominant corporations can afford to do so. Individual standards control only that company's supply chain, so whether they need to be democratically legitimate is arguable. This is especially true when an "exit" option allows suppliers to choose another retailer and consumers to choose other products. In most cases, however, a company that sets and implements its own food standards has a monopsonistic position: it is the supplier's largest or only customer.

McDonald's describes itself as "the world's leading global food service retailer, with more than 33,000 locations serving approximately 64 million customers in 119 countries each day."[27] Its food safety assurance program, arguably the most stringent in the United States and globally in the fast-food industry, has even been used as a model by some government agencies.[28] To change the public perception that it serves "junk food" and to prevent food safety accidents that erode its public image, McDonald's says it has made its corporate food safety and quality assurance program a priority.[29]

Through the program, all products (such as sandwich buns and patties) must be an exact size, color, and temperature, must have the same texture and flavor, and also must undergo regular quality checks throughout the supply chain. Inspections, announced and unannounced, are performed by both internal representatives and third-party auditors. On-site quality assurance staff oversee the production facilities of most suppliers. The company also has a rigorous traceability or tracking system to locate problem areas easily.[30]

Although the company emphasizes collaborative relationships with its suppliers and says suppliers are welcome to contribute ideas and suggestions, McDonald's food safety program is a top-down "take-it-or-leave-it" set of rules. All suppliers, franchisees, and processors of local beef, pork, poultry, dairy, produce, and eggs must meet and maintain McDonald's stringent standards in order to enter and stay in McDonald's kingdom. Standard-setting decisions are made by corporate representatives based on corporate interests, and the rulemaking process is not made public.

Do the McDonald's food standards exemplify private governance as defined earlier? As a leading multinational fast-food retailer, it substantially influences the health and well-being of its 64 million daily customers and the safety policies not only of its competitors but also of governments, especially those in developing countries. To avoid losing investments, for example, the Chinese government has considered strengthening its food safety regulations to catch up with those of Western companies such as Wal-Mart and McDonald's.[31] In this regard, McDonald's food safety and quality assurance program fulfills two of the three criteria that characterize private governance—broad public reach and substantial impact—but does not meet the third criterion, authoritativeness, except within its own supply chain. Its work is not fully accepted by the industry and the public, not used as a court reference, and certainly not implemented and enforced by government agencies, although its operations still dominate and influence the global fast-food market.

Despite their impact, the McDonald's standards might not be expected to be democratically legitimate. Still, when private corporations set the rules, the public's interests are likely to be served only when they coincide with corporate interests. For example, McDonald's did not establish animal welfare standards until 2000 when activists, including People for the Ethical Treatment of Animals (PETA), publicly criticized the treatment of animals by its suppliers. That is, a corporation is likely to respond to public campaigns when profits are at stake. Similarly, other reports suggest that some companies do not take responsibility for any long-term adverse effects of eating their food.[32] Thus the broader social costs and benefits are likely to be ignored and remain as burdens for society.

Collective Food Standards: SQF, GFSI, and GlobalG.A.P.

With regard to private governance and democratic legitimacy, collective food standards are more complicated than individual standards. Collective standards such as those set by SQF, GFSI, and GlobalG.A.P.—industry-led organizations of leading global food retailers—strongly influence the health and well-being of the global public, arguably even more than do the regulations of nations. As more and more large retailers become part of these arrangements, the prominent collective standards become the "rules of the game," appearing to be voluntary but becoming "de facto mandatory" in current global food markets. They become *authoritative* as a tacit agreement among industry participants.

The governance structure and rulemaking process behind collective food standards vary among the different global initiatives, but they share three key similarities: (1) rulemaking authorities are concentrated among major retailers, since they initiate most collective food standards, while other stakeholders are underrepresented; (2) the rulemaking process is not transparent; and (3) systems with two layers—certification and accreditation—help ensure that the standards are consistently met. Standards are certified by private third-party auditing bodies, which are themselves approved by accreditation bodies, also private. Accreditation is "the process by which an authoritative organization gives formal recognition that a particular third-party certifier is competent to carry out specific tasks."[33] Certification verifies that suppliers, including farmers, fishermen, manufacturers, and shippers, follow the letter and the spirit of standards. Third-party certifiers are supposed to be independent of the standard-setter and the entity being examined. Theoretically, then, these systems minimize conflicts of interest. In reality, these seemingly independent accreditors and certifiers depend financially on clients that apply and pay for accreditation and certification, so completely eliminating conflicts of interest is almost impossible.[34]

The Safe Quality Food (SQF) certification is run by the Food Marketing Institute (FMI), a retailer-driven organization established in 1997 when the National Association of Food Chains and the Super Market Institute, both founded in the 1930s, merged.[35] The FMI describes itself as an advocacy body "on behalf of the food retail industry" and represents 75 percent of all retail food stores in the United States (including the world's largest retailer, Wal-Mart). Altogether the FMI consists of more than 1,255 member companies operating in more than fifty countries, though its members are overwhelmingly American.[36] Nearly all members of the FMI board of directors (90 out of 92) represent food retailers and food service providers.[37]

The SQF codes were developed in 1994 by the Ministry of Agriculture of Western Australia, a public agency, but have become worldwide private food standards since the FMI bought the codes in 2003.[38] As a division of the FMI, the Safe Quality Food Institute (SQFI) takes charge of developing and managing the process of certifying that suppliers follow the SQF standards. Participation in this process is quite exclusive, with retailers and wholesalers as the primary actors. Manufacturers and suppliers are underrepresented in the SQFI. Consumers, workers, and civil society organizations, too, have insufficient means to participate.[39] The codes' public origin suggests that their original purpose was to protect public health, not merely to increase corporate profits. Nevertheless, the lopsided representation of retailing and wholesaling interests strongly suggests that their concerns now dominate.

Under the SQFI, there are two additional governance bodies. One is the Technical Advisory Council, composed of industry experts who review SQF standards and make recommendations on training, implementing rules, audits, and certification requirements. Among the twenty-three council members, the plurality are food retailers (eight American and two Australian), and the remaining members represent the accreditation bodies (three), food service operators (four), suppliers (three), the food delivery business (one), and food scholarship (one academic). The other body, the Conference Committee, designs and develops SQF international conferences where major decisions are made.[40]

Figure 5-2 shows the governance network of FMI, which is typical in private food safety governance. Third-party certification bodies have acquired a license agreement with the SQFI to ensure that they provide specified certification services for the SQF, and they must be accredited by an International Accreditation Forum (IAF) accreditation body licensed by FMI.[41] Thus the licensees are tightly controlled by FMI.

The second example of a private governance group in food safety and quality, the Global Food Safety Initiative (GFSI), follows a similar pattern, representing the interests of large corporations, covering approximately 75 to 99 percent of the global food supplies sold by major food retailers.[42] It was established in 2000 in the wake of a series of

FIGURE 5-2. *The Governance Network of the FMI*

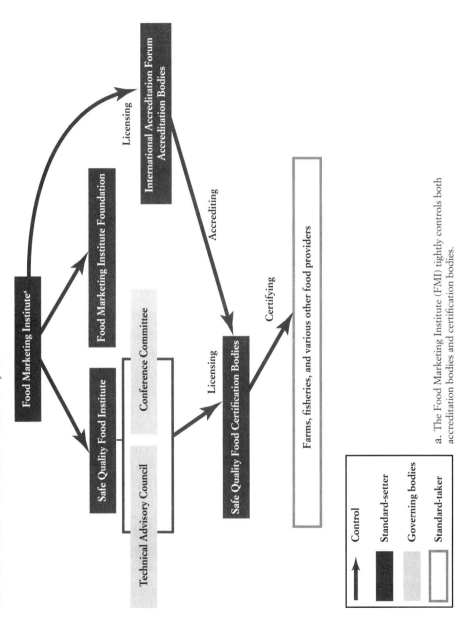

Food Marketing Institute[a]

Food Marketing Institute Foundation

International Accreditation Forum Accreditation Bodies

Safe Quality Food Institute

Conference Committee

Technical Advisory Council

Safe Quality Food Certification Bodies

Farms, fisheries, and various other food providers

Licensing

Accrediting

Licensing

Certifying

Control

Standard-setter

Governing bodies

Standard-taker

a. The Food Marketing Institute (FMI) tightly controls both accreditation bodies and certification bodies.

food safety incidents in an effort to gain "enhanced consumer trust."[43] Meeting at the Consumer Goods Forum (previously the CIES, an international food business network), the CEOs of global retailers decided to launch an organization that would coordinate existing food standards. As a result, instead of generating entirely new food standards, the GFSI develops guidelines that benchmark widely recognized private food standards, including the British Retailer Consortium Global Food Standards for Food Safety, the Dutch Hazard Analysis Critical Control Points (HACCP), the International Food Standards, and the SQF.[44]

The GFSI membership comprises three categories: producers/suppliers, retail and food service, and associates.[45] In an effort to be more inclusive, the GFSI invites participation from other stakeholders as associate members—including certification bodies, standards owners, accreditation organizations, food manufacturers, and civil society organizations—but their influence is limited.[46]

The GFSI Foundation board of directors is the group's main decisionmaking body. Board members are employees of "major global retailers, manufacturers, and food service operators." Most are retailers (thirteen of sixteen in 2011), and board membership is "by invitation only."[47] The GFSI also includes technical working groups whose tasks are mandated by the board and whose members are a "multi-stakeholder group of over 90 food safety experts," including retailers, manufacturers, standard owners, and accreditation and certification bodies.[48] Although these groups are said to be open to all stakeholders, membership is again by invitation only, with the board's approval. Stakeholders such as academics, NGOs, and government representatives can participate in the governance as members of the Advisory Council, but they do not hold decisionmaking authority and play only limited roles. Like SQF, the GFSI relies on third-party certification bodies for enforcement by asking organizations with benchmarked standards to have "contractual and enforceable arrangements" with certification bodies accredited by organizations recognized by the IAF.[49]

The third example of a collective private governance group in food safety and quality is GlobalG.A.P., which originated as EurepGap; it was established to promote "good agricultural practices (GAPs)."[50] GlobalG.A.P. describes itself as "the most widely implemented farm certification scheme worldwide," covering 94,000 suppliers from more than 100 countries.[51] Participation in GlobalG.A.P. is arguably more inclusive than other private food standards groups, as membership is open to a variety of relevant stakeholders such as food retailers, producers, suppliers, NGOs, and other interested groups. Again, members are divided into three groups: retailers, producers/suppliers, and associates "engaged in activities related to the food industry and exercising standardization-related activities."[52] Like the SQF and the GFSI, however, the most influential decisionmakers are retailers and industry leaders from developed countries.

The governance structure of GlobalG.A.P. consists of the board, technical committees, stakeholder committees, certification body committee, and Integrity Surveillance Committee. The board is the main decisionmaking body responsible for "determining strategy, designing the standard-setting procedure, adopting standards and rules, and providing the legal framework for regulating the certification bodies." In an attempt to be more inclusive and fair, the board is made up in equal numbers of producers and retailers, five each, but nine of the ten are from advanced-economy countries. The technical committees, made up of industry experts with equal participation from suppliers and retailers, develop criteria for setting standards and detailed rules. Various stakeholders participate in the stakeholder committees, including members, nonmembers, NGOs, and other stakeholders who, GlobalG.A.P. says, want to be actively involved in the standards development process. However, the stakeholder committees serve only in an advisory and supporting role and are excluded from making important organizational decisions. Also in a supporting capacity, the certification body committee develops proposals and recommendations for the standards development process. In addition, a separate governance body, the Integrity Surveillance Committee, makes final decisions on whether to approve or disqualify certification bodies. Members of this committee, "industry experts with a local legal background," monitor and evaluate the performance of certification bodies approved by GlobalG.A.P. Although it is said to be an independent body, the members are appointed by the board.[53]

GlobalG.A.P. audits of farms are conducted by third-party certification bodies approved by GlobalG.A.P. There are 138 accredited bodies that carry out GlobalG.A.P. certification by conducting both announced and unannounced inspections and audits, suggesting that GlobalG.A.P. takes its work seriously. The care that GlobalG.A.P. takes is underscored by other conditions that certification groups must meet. Under a memorandum of understanding with GlobalG.A.P., the only bodies that are permitted to accredit certification organizations are those that are members of the International Accreditation Forum (IAF) and signatories of the multilateral agreement (MLA) section on product certification. These requirements mean that "the accreditation body (AB) has been subject to a peer evaluation in the product certification field and has received a positive recommendation in its report."[54] In short, these third-party certifiers are likely to be competent. Moreover, by using independent, accredited certifiers GlobalG.A.P. goes to great lengths to remove conflicts of interest between farms and their inspectors.

ASSESSING DEMOCRATIC LEGITIMACY OF COLLECTIVE PRIVATE GOVERNANCE EXAMPLES

These three examples of collective food safety standards can be assessed according to Dingwerth's three criteria for democratic legitimacy: inclusiveness, transparency, and accountability.[55]

Inclusiveness

The predominant initiators and decisionmakers in the three foregoing examples are major food retailers with considerable controlling power throughout their supply chains. Because their prominent private standard-setting initiatives are industry, and, more specifically, retailer-driven organizations, the participation of consumers, workers, small suppliers and producers, and governments is marginal. These other interests, to the degree that they diverge from those of the big retailers, are represented little, if at all, despite their significant stake in food safety and quality.

Private food standards enable some customers—primarily those from industrialized societies—to enjoy higher quality food and enable large retailers to reap advantages such as pre-empting and preparing public regulations, building their reputations, reducing liability risks, and differentiating their products. The burden of this system is borne by those at the bottom of the supply chains. Small producers and processors that cannot meet these standards are likely to suffer the most by losing the opportunity to participate in a possibly important market for them. This imbalance may keep small suppliers on the economic sidelines, especially those in developing countries.[56] Almost by definition, the global food governance system sidelines developing countries, even though they make up a large part of global food markets. Recognizing these deficiencies, a number of NGOs have established their own certification initiatives or have participated in some multi-stakeholder initiatives to work with small producers and suppliers in developing countries, but the influence of these initiatives is meager thus far.[57]

Smaller suppliers and those from developing countries are not the only ones frozen out by private governance dominated by large retailers. The public interest may be served only incidentally or when a sufficiently large affinity group, such as animal rights activists, can embarrass retailers or threaten their profits enough to move them to reform their practices. Those whose concerns are not consistent with retailers' interests must work independently and from the outside for change, a decidedly uphill battle. For these reasons, it seems clear that private food governance fails the inclusiveness test.

Transparency

A lack of transparency in rulemaking further downgrades the democratic legitimacy of private food governance. The process, including standard-setting, implementing standards, and monitoring and verifying that standards are met, are invisible to consumers and the general public, and they are hidden under the mechanism of supply-chain governance.[58] These standards are business-to-business standards operating between participants in the supply chains, not business-to-consumer standards. Although certain food products are labeled, for example, as "SQF certified," consumers are unlikely to know exactly what that means.

In addition, underrepresentation of other stakeholders makes the governance process even less transparent because information is shared only among the members, especially a few major decisionmakers.

Accountability and Conflicts of Interest

Despite the possibility of a principal-agent problem, two processes have been established to make collective private food standard-setters more accountable: accreditation and certification. As seen above, most private food standards are enforced by "independent" third-party certifiers who can be presumed to reduce conflicts of interest and achieve neutrality because they are thought to have no stake in the outcome of an audit.[59] This third-party certification is likely to be more reliable, credible, and therefore more legitimate than first- or second-party certification.

However, the credibility of these third parties is often questioned because of potential conflicts between their desire to be seen as competent regulators and their quest for more paying customers to audit. Some scholars argue that they should be strict enough to be acknowledged as reliable auditors for retailers, and at the same time, lenient enough to attract more suppliers as clients. Similarly, accreditors also have an interest in attracting more certification bodies as clients to generate more income.[60] Moreover, accreditation is sometimes performed by a group designated by the large retailer, suggesting that the accreditor is hardly "independent."

These potential conflicts of interest inherently generate an accountability problem that, like credit raters discussed in the previous chapter, can only be adequately addressed with a shift in the business model that certifiers and accreditors use. The need to attract paying clients creates a potential conflict of interest. Instead of being paid directly by a client who might wish lenient treatment and flee to another provider if the first one is too strict, certifiers and accreditors might use FASB's method of taxing the whole industry to support FASB's operation. That change required a central authority, Congress, to legislate it.[61]

Fair representation of all significant stakeholders is one of the mechanisms that can enhance accountability in governance, but it is virtually nonexistent in private food safety governance. In addition, since safety and quality are the main concerns of private food standards, issues such as workers' welfare, the income and well-being of small producers, and other social implications are likely to be ignored.[62] Little direct accountability to those who are underrepresented, including the general public, is to be found in private governance in these areas.

In sum, private food governance raises serious questions about democratic legitimacy, failing to meet all three criteria. Nevertheless, the public and social impact of private food governance is growing and will continue to grow since global food markets are expanding and becoming more integrated. Moreover, society appears to benefit in many ways with the existence of private food standards, even with the system's democratic deficiencies. Nevertheless, private food standard-setting by retailers, individually and collectively, permits powerful private actors to dominate rulemaking, implementation, and enforcement, which are traditionally seen as the responsibility of public actors.[63]

GROWING PUBLIC RELIANCE ON COLLECTIVE PRIVATE GOVERNANCE

Collective private standards are not merely market instruments for competition; they also influence public laws and regulations.[64] Some advocates of private food standards claim that public food regulations fail to reflect or swiftly respond to market and technological changes, such as an expanding integrated global food market, technical improvements in production and processing methods, and growing public concerns about food production. With a lack of administrative capacity and expertise, policymakers have sought ways to respond appropriately to such changes.[65] Government regulators are in fact increasingly relying upon and thus reinforcing private food standards in their rulemaking.

One example is the U.S. Food Safety Modernization Act (FSMA) of 2011 and its follow-up regulations. According to recently proposed FDA rules under FSMA, the agency should formulate "model accreditation standards" for certification bodies by referring to existing private food standards and accreditation bodies.[66] The success of this law depends greatly on the effectiveness of private food standards and accredited third-party certifications recognized by the FDA, further evidence of the growing governmental reliance on private food standards. Paradoxically, this dependence could lead to a lack of accountability in public regulation and undermine its legitimacy.[67]

In the food, worker safety, and finance areas, among others, government regulations and private standards often complement and reinforce each other. Public regulators and private standard-setters have come to depend on each other in achieving their respective goals.

In the same way that OSHA relies on private groups to make rules pertaining to workplace health and safety, the food safety standards system represents an intermingling of public and private groups. Navigating this system, assessing it, holding responsible parties accountable for their actions and inactions, and influencing rules and their enforcement is a very complicated process about which the average citizen, the press, policy scholars, and most elected officials know little.

THE CONFLUENCE OF PRIVATE AND GOVERNMENT RULEMAKING: MARKETING ORDERS AND AGREEMENTS

A final example of private groups making public policy in food safety and quality in the United States can be found in federal- and state-level marketing orders and marketing agreements. Legally grounded in the 1937 Agricultural Marketing Agreement Act, these are formal instruments—usually initiated by industry and issued by the Agricultural Marketing Services (AMS) of the U.S. Department of Agriculture (USDA)—that place restrictions on the production and/or marketing of a commodity. As the name suggests, marketing orders are mandatory, requiring all individuals and businesses classified as "handlers" of the commodity to comply with the restrictions. Marketing agreements, in contrast, are voluntary but might in practice be less so.[68] Both instruments, reports the FDA, are funded "by assessments levied on handlers and based on the volume of commodity they handle."[69] They are established in the marketing of fruits, vegetables, nuts, milk, and other agricultural commodities for various purposes, including market stabilization, price control, quality standardization, research and development, and regulating advertising practices. Marketing orders fall into the category of hybrid or fourth-arena governance.

By 2014, at the federal level more than thirty marketing orders and no marketing agreements were operative, though several state-level marketing agreements were in place.[70] One example of a federal marketing order involving safety and quality is the one that monitors the deadly bacteria salmonella in almonds (Marketing Order 981: California Almond); another is the limit on aflatoxins (produced by mold) in pistachios (Marketing Order 983: California Pistachio).

Marketing orders are, in general, initiated by industry officials when they identify marketing problems. Once industry supports creating an order, a steering committee of key industry people prepares a proposal, which is submitted to the USDA for review. A USDA administrative law judge presides over a public hearing on the proposal and, based on hearing evidence and follow-up documents, the USDA decides whether to accept the request. If it is accepted and if two-thirds of handlers, either by commodity volume or number of handlers, vote in favor, the marketing order is approved, and it is then administered by a committee of key industry players and one USDA staff member.[71] If an order loses its usefulness, handlers can "vote to dissolve it during one of its periodic continuation votes—usually held every few years."[72] The larger public is entirely excluded from this process; the USDA provides the administrative platform for producers and handlers to develop public policy and the participation of one staff member.

The pistachio marketing order was implemented in 2005 and administered by an eleven-member committee of eight producers, two handlers, and one member of the USDA staff.[73] Intended to reverse the decline in pistachio exports to the European Union, this marketing order requires that all U.S. pistachios be inspected for aflatoxin levels. That order is legally binding and enforceable by the government, demonstrating how marketing orders combine public and private governance. Though small handlers and others that do not target the global market might not benefit from the resulting rules, all producers and handlers, regardless of benefit, are required to pay to support the creation of marketing orders.

Because marketing agreements are voluntary, they even more closely resemble private governance, although their rulemaking procedures are similar to those of marketing orders. One example, different from the major collective food standards examined earlier, is the Leafy Greens Products Handler Marketing Agreement (LGMA), a state-level marketing agreement.

The LGMA was established in 2007 in California after an outbreak of *E. coli* contamination in spinach the previous year.[74] Approximately 200 people across the United States and Canada were sickened; of those, 104 were hospitalized and 31 suffered serious complications. The bacteria were traced to spinach harvested in the Salinas Valley. The FDA took strong action, temporarily banning sales of bagged spinach in stores and restaurants.[75] Leafy greens handlers in California also responded quickly by recommending new standards, audits, and certifications to minimize microbial contamination risks and ensure the safety of leafy green products produced in California.

Although the LGMA is voluntary, nearly 120 shippers and handlers, representing 99 percent of California leafy greens sector, have joined.[76] Since California is the nation's leading producer of leafy greens, the influence of the LGMA rules is substantial. In fact, it became a reference for food safety programs in other states, such as Arizona and Florida.

The LGMA has four rulemaking bodies: the communications committee (seven industry members), the compliance subcommittee (three industry members, two industry alternates, and one public member), the executive committee (seven industry members), and the technical committee (sixteen industry members, one consulting firm representative, and one professional group representative).[77] As these figures indicate, most decisionmakers are producers and packers in the California leafy greens industry, and public participation on the subcommittee is limited to one.

One distinctive feature of the LGMA not typically found in the prominent private collective food standards is its strong enforcement mechanism and close partnership with the California state government. While most private food standards rely on internal audits and third-party certification for enforcement, the California Department of Food and Agriculture (CDFA) monitors the LGMA and verifies compliance. CDFA inspectors, having received USDA training and certification, execute the audits.[78] Almost all growers of leafy greens in California have incorporated LGMA best practices into their written standard operating procedures and regularly document their verification procedures.[79] Noncompliance results in serious punishment, from citations for minor infringement to decertification for repeated violations.[80]

The pistachio marketing order and the LGMA show both the possibilities and the limitations of public-private food governance. First, these cases confirm that in addition to major retailers, other actors in the supply chain such as growers, packers, and shippers can be influential in setting rules, while important stakeholders such as consumers and the general public are not well represented. Second, marketing orders and marketing agreements dealing with food safety and quality are possible only when there is apparent congruence between industry and governmental interests. When products such as leafy greens and pistachios are unbranded, and when the safety and quality issues of these products affect not just a specific supplier but the entire industry, industry-led standards become feasible and effective. Third, these examples partially ease the problems of accountability and transparency since monitoring and enforcement are performed by a government agency and inspection results are publicly available, but it does not solve the issue of democratic legitimacy entirely because the rules are written by self-interested private actors without much public oversight.

CONCLUSION

Private governance in the food sector is similar in many ways to private governance in the financial sector. Public and private regulators often function as partners rather than competitors, with the government largely deferring to private actors, and they are intertwined in developing and enforcing standards. The standards developed by private groups in the two sectors affect the health and finances of the public and specific stakeholders within each industry.

However, one major difference is that most private food standards can be characterized as "supply-chain governance." The power imbalance among participants expresses itself in a unique fashion in that their activities are market driven and can lead to higher, not lower, standards than would be applied by governments. The large food retailers are the *purchasers*, and, because of their concentration in number, they can serve as bridges across the globe, creating and enforcing their own standards, determining standard-setting governance mechanisms, and deciding whose interests are included. Because their standard-setting process is private, it need not be transparent, inclusive of weaker stakeholders, or directly accountable to the public. Many important decisions, such as which products are deemed safe, what is "organic," or how to regulate GMOs, are in the hands of a small number of major retailers rather than the hands of public representatives or a more balanced array of stakeholders.

Do private food standards do a good job of filling governments' regulatory gap? The answer is "partly." They do so only when private interests are congruent with public interests. As explained earlier, consumers' growing concern about food safety and quality has contributed to the development of more stringent private food standards. However, even though consumers in advanced countries have become more enlightened about the potential health and environmental hazards of food, there is little way for them to know exactly how food products are produced and processed because production methods are complex and lack transparency.

In spite of an abundance of public and private food standards, in the United States some food products (that is, ingestible products) have been left unregulated or insufficiently regulated, such as dietary supplements purported to have special health benefits.[81] Some companies take advantage of the lack of transparency and regulatory loopholes by hiding the potential health hazards of their wares. For example, many companies choose not to reveal that their products contain food additives and ingredients that are potentially hazardous because the decades-old U.S. law regarding food additives (the Food Additive Amendment of 1958, of the Food, Drug, and Cosmetic Act of 1938) allows companies to omit listing substances "generally regarded as safe" (GRAS)—a vague phrase left to the interpretation of the seller.[82] GRAS is ill-defined and problematic since, oftentimes, the determination of whether an ingredient is safe is made by "a small group of scientific experts repeatedly hired by companies or consultants with a financial incentive to market new ingredients," according to the Center for Public Integrity, an investigative news organization.[83] Even sophisticated consumers can be unaware of the adverse effects of certain additives and newly developed food products. Finally, poor coordination among private standard-setters creates uncertainty about the safety and quality of food. In the absence of mandatory nationwide regulations on GMO labeling, for example, GMO-free labels have different meanings and reflect different standards.[84]

Despite deficiencies, disentangling the current system would be difficult, perhaps even impossible. The growing inability of the U.S. government to secure food safety and quality in the face of cross-border trade, inadequate resources, and statutory limits on what government agencies are permitted to do has led to an increasing reliance on private groups to make and enforce rules on food safety. This situation seems to be irreversible.

However, permitting and even encouraging private groups to make public policy poses severe challenges to national self-governance "of, by, and for the people." As a practical matter, the democratic legitimacy of private and public-private food governance should be improved by increasing its transparency and broadening the voices involved in policymaking. Governments need to be particularly attentive to the long-term effects of foods, as the profit motive makes private groups more concerned about foods' shorter-term, traceable impact. Lacking proof of actual harm, the U.S. government generally follows a laissez-faire policy in food regulation unless an actual outbreak of food-borne illness is identified. On the assumption that these conditions will continue, we believe that in order to protect public health the government needs to vigorously support scientific research on the possible long-term harm of foods and food production. Government could also ensure wider public representation on government-sponsored bodies and instruments such as those formed for food marketing orders.

Six

PRIVATE GOVERNANCE
IN THE PROFESSIONS AND
HIGHER EDUCATION ACCREDITATION

Two related areas that fundamentally affect the public welfare are higher education accreditation and the advanced professions, such as veterinary medicine, accounting, architecture, law, psychology, pharmacy, dentistry, and medicine. Private policymaking entities flourish within the learned professions.[1] Some represent individuals and some represent organizations to which professionals belong. Traditionally, the rules and policies governing professionals have been made by the professions themselves.[2] Similarly, private self-governing groups, some of them involving the learned professions, decide what standards should be applied to institutions of higher education and whether the standards are being met. These judgments require technical knowledge, but they also entail value choices. The public has a fundamental interest in many of decisions made by professional groups in their governing capacity. Just as demonstrated in the areas of finance and food safety, federal and state governments frequently piggyback on private groups' decisionmaking, defer to professional bodies on major policy decisions, and rely on these organizations to enforce rules, both their own and sometimes those of the government.

For centuries, populations have supported or at least acquiesced to the idea that individuals gain professional status through advanced education and career practice that sets them apart from the general public. In legal scholar John W. Wade's summary of the roots of professionalism in Western history, he quotes several thoughtful observers, including Roscoe Pound and Alexis de Tocqueville.[3] In 1953, Pound, for example, defined a profession as "a group of men pursuing a learned art in the spirit of public services." By dint of their specialized knowledge and skills, professionals are traditionally seen to have obligations to the public. They are also expected to maintain confidential relationships with their clients and to hold themselves to a demanding ethical code of performance. And they are supposed to put the interests of the client and the public above their own. One hundred years before Pound, Alexis de Tocqueville observed the role of one group of professionals—lawyers—in maintaining what is today called civil society. In *Democracy in America,* he said that lawyers and the influence they exert were "the most powerful existing security against the excesses of democracy, supplying the sobriety and stability, which every good society requires."

Professions regulate themselves through self-governing nonprofit organizations. For instance, lawyers define, administer, and even police the legal profession through state bar associations and the American Bar Association, which is composed exclusively of lawyers certified to practice in one or more states. Similarly, through their national and state associations physicians define acceptable practice in medicine and specify who should be permitted to practice. In both law and medicine, states put their imprimatur on standards set by these private governance societies. In medicine, professional rulemaking groups exist for nearly all aspects of medical practice and almost every part of the human body. Most of these groups are professional societies, though some are not, such as the ever-expanding Joint Commission on Accreditation of Healthcare Organizations, which accredits more than 20,000 health facilities.[4] In an earlier incarnation, the Joint Commission arose from efforts of a professional society, the American College of Surgeons, which established minimum standards for hospitals beginning in 1917. Today five organizations are corporate members of the Joint Commission: the American Hospital Association, the American Medical Association, the American College of Physicians, the American College of Surgeons, and the American Dental Association. The latter four are professional societies. Without accreditation from the Joint Commission, health care organizations ranging from hospitals to specialized surgery centers to home health care agencies cannot receive Medicare or Medicaid reimbursement. Nor will private insurers reimburse patients served by organizations not accredited by this private group whose board includes only a handful of nominally public members.

Another category of professionals, engineers, wields policymaking powers over matters that affect public safety. They are organized into several general and specialized groups. One of the largest is the National Council of Examiners for Engineering and Surveying (NCEES).[5] This body certifies that an individual is trained according to the council's specifications and is capable of designing and overseeing the construction of highways, bridges, dams, buildings, and other major facilities used by the public every day. The public has much riding on the policies made by this organization and other engineering societies.

While the groups of professionals engaged in public policymaking vary in many ways, they share some fundamental characteristics. The most important of these features is autonomy. Eliot Freidson, a leading student of professionalism, summarizes the situation aptly: "The formal institutions of professionalism establish the economic and social conditions which allow those with a specialized body of knowledge and skill to control their own work."[6]

The premise underlying the independence of professionals is that they are highly trained in specialized areas that require them to exercise judgment and require the public to trust them. The right to exercise judgment is based on many years of education—via a curriculum

PUBLIC POLICYMAKING BY PRIVATE ORGANIZATIONS

developed by senior specialists in the field—and then certification by accredited institutions and standardized, challenging examinations. All practitioners of a profession must undergo such training and must continue their education throughout their careers to keep their skills and knowledge current. Professional associations determine the content of education and qualifying examinations, conduct accreditation of teaching institutions, make rules, and adjudicate cases of their possible violation. However, they also perform nonpolicymaking activities ranging from lobbying governments on issues of interest to publishing peer-reviewed journals, holding meetings, and organizing continuing education.

Freidson explains that professionals have accrued their power through persuasion. The professions start out with no intrinsic economic or political power. Over time, they convince the public that their dominance is necessary, legitimate, and beyond the reach of political or representative institutions. They are beyond reach because only they have the training and experience to make policy in their specialties. Their powers rest in part on the acquiescence of the public and of governments that rely on them. Through their self-governing organizations, they engage in public policymaking functions, even though those functions are not typically recognized as public policymaking. However, the autonomy of the professions has been curtailed in recent decades owing largely to their growing dependence on federal government support—often indirect, through student grants and loans and government-provided health insurance, for example.

The exceptional policymaking power of professional societies raises questions about their democratic legitimacy. That professional expertise is indispensable in making reasonable and savvy policy does not provide adequate justification for private groups to make what is, for all intents and purposes, public policy.[7] To what degree are professional policymaking procedures transparent and inclusive, and to whom are professional bodies ultimately accountable? Is reliance on professional groups to make and enforce policy an abdication of the government's responsibility in a democracy? When do purely technical determinations spill over into the realm of value choices that should be under the purview of those affected by those choices? Is it even possible for average citizens to be represented in this policymaking, which can substantially influence their life and well-being, when nearly all policy decisions are made by an organization's members without much, if any, visibility or public input? And, are there ways to increase public participation while maintaining high-quality decisions and not undercutting professional autonomy in a way that harms the larger society?

The huge amount of public money supporting the work of some professions has opened the door for the government to make demands on what professionals do and what they can charge for their services if they accept government funds, among other matters. Such government intrusion can be justified to the degree that government's demands on professional groups reflect the public's value choices, including how to spend its taxes and what matters most to the general populace. It also seems reasonable for government to reach into professional practices sufficiently to outlaw conflicts of interest and practices, such as racial discrimination, that run contrary to the overall policy (and values) of the country. However, government intrusion can undermine the very concept of a learned profession: its autonomy and the exercise of reasoned judgment by professionals.[8]

The bodies that represent professionals are the most capable of defining and certifying their qualifications for practice. Thriving, independent professional societies are consistent with the concept of limited government in a flourishing civil society. However, sometimes the interests of the public and those of professional groups are not clearly aligned, particularly when the decisions of these bodies have the force of law, as in the case of setting reimbursement rates for doctors (as explained below). In such cases, specific avenues are needed to ensure that public interests are served. The need for expertise does not obviate either the possibility or the normative desirability of democratic legitimacy. What is needed is balance among these concerns and care in dividing responsibilities between government and professional groups. When delegating policymaking authority to private groups, governments have an obligation to exercise vigilant oversight of the procedures used to arrive at decisions and the content of the decisions to ensure that public interests are served.

An old bromide in representative governance notes that in public policymaking there is "no pancake that does not have two sides." The role of professionals in policymaking bears this saying out. The public needs highly trained professionals. Professionals must have the freedom to build and govern their societies and to exercise their best judgment when practicing their craft. They have the expertise needed in specialized policymaking and in their practice, but it is difficult to rationalize this power with the basic tenets of democratic legitimacy. The variations among professional groups—in their rulemaking procedures, the composition of their governing boards, their structure and relationships with governments—limit glib generalizing about them and merit the examination of specific groups. Two areas, higher education accreditation and rulemaking in medicine, are investigated here in more detail.

HIGHER EDUCATION ACCREDITATION: A HIERARCHY OF INSTITUTIONS

The role of the U.S. government in accrediting academic institutions grew dramatically after World War II. Before that time Congress had virtually no interest in regulating higher education.[9] By 1944, Congress was preparing for the return of millions of troops demobilizing after World War II by enacting the GI Bill of Rights, or more formally the Serviceman's Readjustment Act of 1944. This legislation provided home loan, education, and unemployment benefits to those veterans. One result was a huge increase in the number of students enrolled in colleges and universities. By 1947, veterans made up almost half of college admissions, according to the U.S. Veterans Administration.[10] The enrollment deluge continued over the next decade, and by 1956 about half of the 16 million returning veterans had taken advantage of the education benefits.

Today the United States enrolls nearly 70 percent of high school graduates in some form of post-secondary education. Nearly everyone with a high school diploma can find a seat somewhere in an accredited institution of higher education. In 2014, nearly 20 million students were enrolled.[11] The federal government plays a major role in funding higher education for everyone through student loans and grants. In 2014, students received almost $30 billion in grants (Pell grants) and $100 billion in new loans, adding to the $1.2 trillion in student debt.[12] Federal research funding directed to higher education institutions was approximately $134 billion.[13] Little wonder that both administrators at the U.S. Department of Education and elected officials want to know whether those dollars are spent wisely.

Some oversight is in place, as Congress and state legislatures exercise financial oversight of appropriated funds. State governments partially finance public universities and colleges and are responsible for licensing all institutions of higher education within their borders, both public and private, presumably providing some level of surveillance.[14] Yet government bodies traditionally have had little or nothing to say about the core functions of higher education institutions, namely, what is taught (the content of courses within the curriculum), who is qualified for admission, who has met the requirements for graduation and is eligible to receive a degree, and who is hired, promoted, and tenured as faculty.

In higher education, for a government to interfere with these core functions would impede the maintenance of democracy and the freedoms that underlie it. Left to their own devices, governments have an interest in controlling certain versions of history or dismissing iconoclasts, for example. Universities controlled by faculty help prevent such interference and help ensure democratic freedoms.[15] At the same time, faculty may have little interest in engaging in activities that government officials expect, such as spending its money in the most efficient fashion, making sure that enrolled students actually graduate, or teaching effectively. Sometimes values clash, such as when professors want and need (for reasons of professional advancement) to emphasize their research over their undergraduate teaching duties. At other times disagreements are empirical, such as over whether it is possible to measure the outcomes of spending on higher education in a meaningful fashion.

However, professors are not given carte blanche to do what they want. While they determine the core functions at their institutions (often in concert with their academic professional societies), their universities are subject to review by a highly developed system, anchored by self-governing accrediting agencies. State public universities are subject to decisions by boards that have been appointed by governors, a practice that can intrude on academic freedoms and control.

The accrediting "agencies"—they are private—are created and funded by universities. The accreditors act as private policymakers in higher education: they set basic standards for what graduate and undergraduate institutions should do and determine whether their performance is adequate, given each institution's goals and self-assessment. And universities must demonstrate to accreditors that they have the financial strength to deliver high-quality academic programs to students.

In addition to the accrediting agencies, the system includes the Council for Higher Education Accreditation (CHEA), a not-for-profit association whose members are three thousand of the almost eight thousand accredited degree-granting institutions in the United States (see table 6-1). This organization recognizes and reviews sixty of the institutional and programmatic accrediting organizations at ten-year intervals, and it holds training sessions for those who work for accrediting agencies as volunteers or paid employees and reviews standards for the accrediting work performed by accreditors.[16]

TABLE 6-1. *Academic Institutions Accredited in 2012–13 by Recognized Accrediting Organizations*

Type of institution	Number
Regional	3,049
National faith-related	503
National career-related	4,344
Total	7,896

Source: Council for Higher Education Accreditation at http://chea.org/Almanac%20Online/index.asp.

Oversight of universities through private accreditation, then, is both considerable and arguably onerous, as further described below. It relies largely on the integrity of professors, higher education institutions, and the accreditors that are overseen by those institutions in an essentially self-referential system that invites little public involvement. Nevertheless, governments can influence quite substantially what universities do.

GOVERNMENT INVOLVEMENT

Generally, governments have accepted the notion that self-regulation is probably the best approach to sustaining quality in higher education and that education professionals should be the key decisionmakers about academic matters.[17] However, trust in the system has eroded somewhat in recent years, as has the autonomy of higher education.

The acceptance of self-governance is reflected in the fact that the federal government requires a college to be accredited in order to be eligible to receive federal monies, either directly for research or indirectly from students who pay their tuition with government grants and loans. Even the wealthiest of institutions would likely be forced to close if they lost their accreditation. In the case of the wealthy institu tions, the importance of being accredited is not only a question of receiving government monies.[18] Accreditation also is a matter of cre- dentialing and prestige. Were students to graduate from an unaccred- ited school, most employers and others would not see their degrees as valuable or even valid. Consequently, it is rare that a degree-granting institution in the United States is not accredited by one of the private accrediting organizations.[19]

To fulfill its fiduciary responsibilities in higher education, the U.S. Department of Education, while not interfering directly in academic decisions made by universities, received congressional authority to li- cense all accrediting agencies, creating yet another layer of administra- tion and providing a point of entry for government involvement in higher education.[20] The National Advisory Committee on Institutional Quality and Integrity (NACIQI), established in 1972, reviews all li- censed accreditors every ten years through a process not unlike the process that accreditors themselves have established for accrediting in- stitutions of higher education (described below). NACIQI has eighteen members, appointed in equal numbers, six each, by the secretary of education, the House of Representatives, and the Senate, potentially politicizing accreditation but also potentially giving the public an indi- rect way to influence accreditation and the priorities of universities.

For the first twenty-five years of NACIQI's history, it reviewed ac- creditors primarily on the fairness of their operations. It acted as a buffer between higher education and government, so that profession- als could control academic matters without government interference.[21] The most important questions asked of accrediting agencies in those years were about due process and whether accrediting agencies were somehow discriminating against institutions in ways that would violate it.

Though private in form, accrediting agencies accede to the wishes of government officials when they are expressed with sufficient persis- tence and force. Beginning in the early twenty-first century, the Department of Education began to use NACIQI to force policy changes in educational institutions themselves. The department was looking for ways to improve quality in higher education, but Congress would not, or did not, give it the authority to define quality directly. So the department began to insist that accrediting agencies require measures of quality assessment and include an appraisal of outcomes as a part of their accreditation reviews. For example, universities are asked by the accrediting agencies to measure how much students learn over the course of their degree programs. The practical problems associated with quantifying what students learn have aroused considerable opposition in universities. Doing so is perceived not only as impractical, and maybe impossible, in the post-secondary context but also as an unwarranted intrusion by government that seems to erode the centrality of professional judgment.[22] In any case, meaningful measurement of outcomes has yet to be achieved.

In another area, the accreditation of for-profit colleges, the federal government pressed hard for a change in the accreditation process, especially by the academically oriented regional accreditors (discussed below). The well-organized for-profit education industry apparently wanted not only the respectability that accreditation provided but also access to federal student grant and loan money, a goal which they have achieved.[23] To understand this conflict, a little history is needed.

In 1972 the Higher Education Amendments stated that for-profit institutions could receive government funds. Twenty years later the House of Representatives Committee on Education and the Workforce indicated that for-profit institutions would normally have student-aid eligibility. With this congressional endorsement of profit-making higher education schools, for-profits proliferated. However, they needed accreditation. Regional accreditors were quite reluctant to bring for-profits within their fold. To accommodate this need, the Accrediting Council for Independent Colleges and Schools (ACICS) and the American Commission of Career Schools and Colleges (ACCSC)—nonprofit organizations established in 1912 and 1965, respectively, for the purpose of accrediting occupational and technical education—provided certification of these new for-profits, many of which delivered their programs exclusively online.[24] In contrast, the more academically rigorous regional accreditors were quite reluctant to consider accreditation for proprietary colleges.[25] Regionally accredited institutions will not typically accept transfer credits from schools accredited by the ACICS or the ACCSC.[26]

Because some well-placed members of Congress and officials in the Department of Education implied that the government would no longer rely on the existing accreditors if the for-profits were excluded, not recognizing them would have threatened the central role of the regional and other academic accreditors and perhaps their very existence. Given the support for market-driven activities in this country and the existence of some high-quality for-profit institutions, it seemed unreasonable for accreditors to exclude the for-profit schools.[27] The academic accreditors changed course. Now a number of the larger, well-known for-profit institutions are included in the regional accreditors' membership, and they are judged by the same standards as the not-for-profit sector.[28] Was the attitude toward non-profits a case of conflict of interest or a conflict of values? Probably both. Though the accrediting organizations are large, monopolistic bureaucracies, their members and base of support were exclusively the nonprofit universities, which did not want proprietary colleges to operate on their terrain. However, the regionals' opposition to accrediting profit making colleges were well-founded, given their overall poor performance.[29]

HOW HIGHER EDUCATION ACCREDITATION WORKS

Each year thousands of academic institutions and programs undergo accreditation review (see table 6-1). Academic institutions in the United States have very diverse missions. Some have religious missions; some are nondenominational. Some are committed to the liberal arts, and some are more vocationally oriented. Most are not-for-profit, both public and private; others are set up as for-profit institutions governed by corporate-like boards of directors or are individually owned and operated.

Pluralism is one of the cornerstones of higher education in the United States, and governments make no judgments about educational aims. Accreditors, too, accept that position and do what they can to help an institution achieve the objectives that it has set for itself. Accreditors in the United States have the authority to insist on changes and even withdraw an institution's accreditation, but their major concern is strengthening their member institutions, not closing their doors.[30]

The most visible and largest of the accrediting organizations are the six "regionals," including the Higher Learning Commission, with 1,337 member colleges and universities in the Midwest, and the Middle States Commission on Higher Education, with 528 member institutions in the Northeast, to give two examples.[31] The regional associations organize reviews of all its colleges and universities in ten-year cycles. If, however, a warning has been issued by an agency based on a school's failure to meet its standards in previous accreditation processes, a review is undertaken sooner, usually within a year or two, to determine if those deficiencies have been remedied.

Founded in 1885, the regional New England Association of Schools and Colleges makes its oversight mission clear in its statement of standards for accreditation. The titles of the eleven standards it uses to judge an institution represent what most accreditors look at when they visit an institution: Mission and Purposes, Planning and Evaluation, the Academic Program, Faculty, Students, Library and Other Information Resources, Physical and Technological Resources, Financial Resources, and Public Disclosure and Integrity. The institution must elaborate on each standard in detail.[32]

The process followed by all the regionals begins with detailed submissions by the institution, usually more than a year in preparation,

TABLE 6-2. *Accreditation Teams, Volunteers, and Volunteer Financial Support in 2012–13*

Accrediting organization type	Total volunteers available[a]	Number of volunteers who served	Volunteer financial support ($)[b]
Regional	19,162	4,314	4,153,397
National faith-related	1,051	463	180,000
National career-related	5,407	3,023	6,279,125
Programmatic	28,741	11,874	13,170,450
Totals	54,361	19,674	23,782,972

a. Accrediting organizations rely on volunteers in the higher education community and the public to carry out the important function of peer review. In general, these volunteers are unpaid and serve on visiting teams, accreditation decisionmaking bodies, and other task forces or committees of accrediting organizations.

b. Volunteers' honoraria and travel expenses are often provided by the institutions that they are visiting.

Source: Council for Higher Education Accreditation at http://chea.org /Almanac%20Online/index.asp.

followed by site visits, which are paid for by the university. Those on the front lines of the accrediting process, the teams visiting the school for about one week, are faculty selected from other institutions by the accrediting agency. Over 4,000 volunteers made accreditation visits for the regionals in the academic year 2012–13 (see table 6-2). Most were professionals in the fields they were asked to assess. Occasionally a representative of an institution's student body or the public is included, but not often. This process is a quintessential model of self-regulation. (See box 6-1 for a more detailed description.)

After examining institutions to determine how well they live up to their own claims and aspirations, accreditors recommend improvements. Because losing accreditation can be a death knell for a school or program, agencies rarely withdraw recognition altogether and instead call for improvements and re-examination in the near term. This approach honors the tradition of peer review and pluralism in higher education.

On rare occasions, however, loss of accreditation can occur quite dramatically and very much in the public eye. In 2013, the Accrediting Commission for Community and Junior Colleges (ACCJC) gave the City College of San Francisco one year to comply with changes mandated by the commission. Otherwise it would lose its accreditation and be forced to close its doors to its 72,000 students. College officials applied for a two-year extension of the deadline. Simultaneously, the city sued the commission. Despite the community college's putative deficiencies and its many missed opportunities to improve before the ACCJC's pronouncement, enormous political (and judicial, if only because a suit was filed) pressure was placed on the commission to relent, rather than for the school to improve its performance. The accrediting agency acquiesced and gave the college two years to comply with its requirements. The college remained open, and as of February 2016 the legal case against ACCJC is pending.[33] This example shows that sufficient public and political pressure on an accrediting agency can compel it to withdraw its independent judgment.

Rather than withdrawing accreditation, however, much more typical is an accreditor's report that mandates areas in which an institution should make changes that accreditors then will look for in the next visit. It is uncommon, but accreditors do occasionally recommend to the Department of Education that a school's accreditation be withdrawn, which would amount to closing it if the department agreed. A case in point is Southeastern University in Washington, D.C., which was established by an act of Congress in 1879 and in later years was accredited by the Middle States Association. The agency repeatedly noted Southeastern's deficiencies over several years and finally, in summer 2009, withdrew its accreditation on the grounds of financial instability and lack of academic rigor. Critics of the accreditation process argue that Middle States should have pulled the plug years

BOX 6-1. *Typical Steps Followed by Regional Accreditors in the Accreditation Process*

The institution is required to write a self-evaluation and assess itself against the qualitative standards of the accrediting agency. The self-evaluation covers most aspects of a university's operations. The standards themselves are set out in a lengthy document and range from institutional financial viability, to curriculum, faculty and student performance. Usually each department and school within the university writes an evaluation of its programs. This process generally takes more than one calendar year.

A visiting team selected by the accrediting agency receives and studies the university's report and then makes a visit to the campus for a period of at least one week. The number of members in a team is in the range of 15 to 30 people. Many have received training in sessions run throughout the years to better prepare people in the processes of evaluation. (In table 6-2, CHEA estimates that more than 19,000 individuals selected from a pool of more than 54,000 participated in these reviews as volunteers in one year.) During that week the report is discussed with faculty, students, staff and trustees. The teams sent on accrediting visits are usually composed of faculty, staff and sometimes students and public members. Most members of the review team are peers, that is faculty from other academic institutions. The visiting team after a period of some months writes a report to the accrediting agency reporting on their visit and recommending full or partial approval for re-accreditation.

earlier.[34] But the critics ignored two important points. One is that accreditation is meant to foster a diversity of institutions and to help strengthen them, a process that can take some years. Second, closing an institution is politically difficult. Elected officials are loath to passively accept the closing of institutions in their jurisdictions for many

Often the report contains recommendations and suggestions for improvement.

The Board of the accrediting agency reviews the report and makes a decision granting accreditation on a full, partial or conditional basis. The Boards have some public members, a few administrators but faculty mostly populates them.

Governments accept the review of the accrediting agencies and abide by their recommendations. If a university is put on warning for some reason, their federal monies (and existence) is threatened unless the identified insufficiencies are corrected within a given time period.

Public comments are allowed after the accrediting agency makes its decision. The conditions under which an agency will accept a public comment are limited. For example, the Northeast accrediting agency (the nation's largest) has nine criteria a complaint must meet before it will be considered. They include that it must focus on general institutional conditions not individuals, cite specific Standards or Criteria for accreditation put forth by the agency, demonstrate that a serious effort has been made to resolve the issue within the institution and provide full disclosure of any external avenues of complaint are being pursued.

CHEA describes the accrediting process as "a trust-based, standards-based, evidence-based, judgment-based, peer-based process."

Source: Information and quote from Judith S. Eaton, "An Overview of U.S. Accreditation," August 2012, pp. 4–5 (www.chea.org/pdf/Overview%20 of%20US%20Accreditation%202012.pdf).

reasons, not the least of which is that often, especially in smaller communities, colleges and universities contribute to the local culture, can be politically influential, and generate support for the local economy.[35] On balance, shuttering colleges is probably as repugnant to legislators as it is to accreditors, but for different reasons.

While the regionals examine the whole institution, the programmatic or professional associations such as the American Bar Association and the Association of American Law Schools are organized by profession, similar to those in health care areas. These groups evaluate specific programs and schools within universities. It is not uncommon for a major university to have a dozen accrediting organizations overseeing its programs. Like the professional programs, faith-related institutions enjoy their own accreditors, as do career schools, discussed above (see table 6-2).

DEMOCRATIC LEGITIMACY AND HIGHER EDUCATION ACCREDITATION

As the examples here demonstrate, government involvement in accreditation can be sporadic and lopsided, arising when an agency threatens to withdraw its approval of a specific institution or when the agencies do not respond to strongly held positions of government officials. However, political pressure to keep a poor-quality or financially failing institution open degrades higher education and short-changes its students. Likewise, trying to impose outcomes-based indicators may be ill-considered and even destructive of the missions of some institutions, reducing the pluralism of this sector. Even so, private accreditors, while frequently slow to move, sometimes acquiesce. Why? They fear that the government will replace them and make them irrelevant if they do not cooperate. One could argue, however, that their responsiveness to government's demands brings the private accreditors closer to the public's interests, to the degree that the government is representing those interests.

The federal government, however, does not offer the only path to know about or to have its interests represented. Accrediting organizations do provide for limited public participation. The nineteen-member board of the Higher Education Commission (HEC) provides an example. Board members reside within and outside its midwestern jurisdiction. Fourteen are academics or former academics from a variety of institutions, and seven of the fourteen are or have been academic presidents, including three at community colleges. One member is a co-founder of the for-profit DeVry Education Group. Those who might be considered "public" members are a former Kansas state senator, a Kansas Board of Regents member, and two representatives of the business community. It can be argued that these public members contribute a perspective from outside of traditional academia. (And the breadth of institutions, sectors, academic fields, and geography represented on the HEC would seem to limit conflicts of interest in the HEC's accrediting activities and to include a variety of perspectives.) Nevertheless, this effort at public representation, to the extent that it exists, suffers from what plagues virtually all efforts to include the public in private governance. It is nonspecific and nonaccountable. It lacks much, if any, clear meaning. Still, it may broaden the number of concerns brought to bear on an issue.

With regard to transparency, the work of accrediting agencies is not particularly visible to the press and public. For example, controversy exists over whether written reviews of institutions should be made public. The agencies argue that if access to full reports were unrestricted, the visiting professionals who write them would be reluctant to be negative, fearing personal or even legal retaliation and harm to the institution under review. Usually, at least the summaries of reports are available, as are the recommendations, positive and negative, of the reviewing team. Accrediting procedures on campus encourage the participation of all stakeholders, including faculty, students, administrators, trustees, alumni, and the general public in the review process. Still, the work of accreditors goes largely unnoticed outside of academe, largely because it is complex and may seem esoteric.

At the state level, as demands for more oversight and harmonization of publicly funded higher education institutions arose in the

1950s and 1960s, governments established agencies, sometimes called buffer bodies, to coordinate and, in part, shield higher education institutions from direct political intervention while still responding to the need for fiscal and strategic oversight. These buffer bodies, which traditionally are one step removed from governors and legislatures, operate as quasi-independent government commissions that exert a light hand in program oversight. This light hand touches mostly on questions related to expenditure; for example, should a university be allowed to build a medical school or does the state need an additional Ph.D. program in economics? The proceedings of the buffer bodies are available to legislators and the public. And there are accommodations for public participation in their activities. However, most of the people who participate in these proceedings are professionals from the academic community.

As in finance and food safety, the picture of private governance in higher education accreditation is blurred, and many of its elements run contrary to principles of democratic legitimacy. What has been a private system is increasingly being encroached upon by government, a development with both good and bad aspects. On the negative side, one might say that higher education accreditation has been hijacked by the federal government. Matters that arguably should be kept separate from government intervention are not. On the positive side, the involvement of government officials in accreditation provides a route for the public to influence higher education. After all, the government's considerable investment in education is funded by the taxpayers, and they deserve to know and influence how their money is spent.

One could argue that the extensive accreditation process itself constitutes a form of accountability to the public. Accreditation exists to ensure that institutions of higher education meet certain minimum academic standards and engage in practices that comport with each school's claims about what it does. Accreditation shows whether a college has the capacity to live up to its declarations as well as whether it does. The original purpose of this process was to help schools meet their aspirations, not to assist governments with their purposes.

RULEMAKING IN MEDICINE

Among the abundant professional rulemaking groups in the medical community, the American Medical Association (AMA) is the most visible. Founded in 1847, the AMA plays a central role in setting standards for entry into practice and in the ongoing performance of health care professionals. It and its affiliates develop and control standards for medical education and practice in the United States. However, it is worth noting that only 15 percent of practicing physicians belong directly to the AMA, though they are connected indirectly through their medical specialty associations or other linked but independent organizations.[36]

The AMA does its education policy work through an affiliated organization called the Liaison Committee on Medical Education (LCME).[37] The LCME is a programmatic accrediting organization recognized by the Department of Education. In the medical professions, individuals who practice must earn degrees from academic institutions approved by one of the accrediting bodies recognized by the LCME. In medicine and the health professions (and in some other professions, such as the law), accrediting agencies, in cooperation with state governments, then issue licenses for individuals to practice in their specialties. The private organizations of health care professionals, such as the AMA, the College of Physicians, the College of Surgeons, and scores of other national medical associations, put their stamp of approval on individuals who successfully complete a course of study at an accredited medical school, pass a national exam, and meet other requirements. State governments, recognizing the credentialing standards set by the associations, license an individual to practice in their states. Adequately representing the public in professional licensing is difficult both conceptually and in practice. The structure of the AMA

141

and its governing board lacks transparency, and the public's role in its decisionmaking is almost nonexistent.

The AMA is at the heart of the medical professional system and is the place where the public might best participate in medical policymaking. The AMA's members are virtually all practicing professionals in medicine. A few nonmedical professionals are included in its decisionmaking bodies but in very limited numbers. Partially reflecting the federalist structure of the United States, the AMA reports that it is "composed of individual members who are represented in the House of Delegates through state associations and other constituent associations, national medical specialty societies and other entities."[38] A twenty-one-member board of trustees of its House of Delegates governs the AMA itself. Only one trustee is designated to be a member of the public from outside the medical profession. The 500-member Board of Delegates, selected by professional, medicine-related organizations, is the AMA's legislative and policymaking body. Five of the delegates are appointed from the medical services of the federal government. Who or what they represent—their agencies, their specialties, or the larger public—is unknown. The AMA does allow observers at its meetings, which makes this organization more transparent than some private governance bodies. The AMA-affiliated LCME's nineteen-member board overseeing medical education includes only one nonmedical professional.

The AMA's mission statement, which prominently features its ethical precepts, asserts that the association "will build on its legacy of leading physician ethics, setting standards for medical education, and advancing medical science to serve as the premier voice for the core values of the medical profession."[39] Nevertheless, with the overwhelming dominance of medical professionals in rulemaking, whenever the collective interests of medical professionals clash with public concerns, the interests of the professionals are likely to prevail. Such was the case when the AMA fought the establishment of Medicare for senior citizens in the mid-1960s. As a group lobbying the government, the AMA had every right to oppose Medicare, but its opposition is evidence that the AMA's interests and those of the public are not always aligned. The conflict seemed to be between the profession's perceived autonomy and financial well-being and the public's interest in broader medical coverage and lower costs for the disabled and elderly. While the AMA had legitimate concerns about the impact of Medicare on physicians' independence and the capacity of the medical system to absorb new demand while maintaining quality of care, in the end the decision to adopt the legislation—ultimately a matter of values, not technical knowledge—belonged to the public, not the AMA. Correctly, the public, through its representative government, made the decision and the Social Security Act Amendments became law in 1965.

Another example of a possible conflict of interest between professionals and the public is the role of an AMA-selected committee in setting reimbursement rates to medical professionals for Medicare and Medicaid services. The Centers for Medicare and Medicaid Services (CMS) of the U.S. Department of Health and Human Services accepts an estimated 90–95 percent of the "recommendations" of the thirty-one-member Specialty Society Relative Value Scale Update Committee (RUC).[40] Private insurers typically follow suit, with the result that this committee almost unilaterally determines how much doctors are paid for performing various medical procedures.

The formula used is based on the estimated time (from physician surveys) and the presumed level of expertise needed in each category of care. The formula appears to be neutral and empirically solid. But analysis of physicians' bills shows that, according to the formula's time estimate, some practitioners are working more than twenty-four hours a day and at least one procedure, colonoscopy, may be overvalued by as much as 500 percent.[41] Even if the time estimates were corrected, the formula is deeply value laden and influences medical students to choose highly specialized fields that are much better paid than less specialized but nevertheless greatly needed areas of practice. The time of a neurologist, for example, is weighted as fifty times more valuable than that of a general practitioner, usually an internist. It should be noted that most RUC members are specialists.

The implications for the public interest are significant. Why does the United States have a shortage of primary care physicians? Look to the AMA's committee for one answer. Why do health care costs continue to rise? Although it is only one element of a complicated problem, the RUC may be a culprit by continuing to raise specialists' reimbursement rates. Why do seniors have difficulty finding a primary care physician who accepts Medicare? Perhaps it is because the Medicare reimbursements to primary care physicians are so much lower than the reimbursements to specialists. The RUC demonstrates the conflict of interest between public and private concerns that can be present in private policymaking.

The RUC not only makes public policy but also until recently has been largely opaque in its operations. In 2013, however, it began "publishing minutes, dates and locations of meetings, and votes for individual current procedural (CP) codes, though individual votes will not be revealed."[42] In addition, meetings are open to public observers, although they must, according to the AMA website, register first.

Needless to say, most of the public is unaware of the existence of the RUC, and most would not have the time, even if they had the inclination, to observe its work directly. But the press, policy experts, and Congress should be observing and translating this work for the broader public. At the least, closer oversight of CMS in its acceptance of RUC decisions is warranted.

THE ROLE OF THE STATES

State licensing boards enter the policymaking picture cautiously to put a government, and hence a public, imprimatur on the work of state professional associations in the health care field. New York state offers a typical example of the care a government takes to maintain and support yet not interfere with the substantive work of health care professionals.[43] By inference, the state's role is to grant licenses, without inserting itself directly in the decisionmaking processes of the primary professional players. The professionals determine who is eligible for a license, and the state board concurs. The state represents the public, but it recognizes that what professionals do is beyond its competence and that of the general public. In New York, on the recommendation of the commissioner of education, the semi-independent Board of Regents (composed of seventeen unsalaried members elected by the state legislature for five-year terms) appoints a state board for each of the licensed professions. In this two-tiered process, the Board of Regents appoints twenty-nine professional boards to advise it and the State Department of Education on licensing and other regulatory matters such as disciplinary decisions.

Each state board is composed primarily of licensed professionals in the field in which licensing decisions are being made. All New York state boards have at least one public or lay member. In the case of the New York State Board of Medicine, out of a total minimum membership of twenty-four, state law mandates that at least two be members of the public and twenty be physicians (of whom at least two are physician assistants and two licensed physicians who hold a Doctor of Osteopathic medicine [D.O.]).

All states have similar licensing organizations. In addition to licensing, state medical boards oversee the proper conduct of medical physicians, thus providing the public a point of access to this part of medical decisionmaking. Again using New York as an example, the Department of Health's Office of Professional Medical Conduct (OPMC) investigates complaints that are made against physicians for "failure of a licensed professional to meet expected standards of practice."[44] If the office finds credible evidence of misconduct, the State Board of Professional Medical Conduct will hear the evidence and determine what, if any, penalty will apply. The OPMC reported in its 1997 annual report that:

Physicians are involved in every stage of the discipline process, from assessing the initial complaint to hearing the appeal of a disciplined physician. OPMC has 24 full- and part-time staff physicians. These physicians work with investigators, many of whom are nurses, to evaluate allegations of misconduct. A wide spectrum of medical specialties is represented by the OPMC roster of medical coordinators.[45]

Most members of the staff of the OPMC are physicians. Two-thirds of the members of the State Board for Professional Medical Conduct are physicians appointed by the governor on the recommendation of medical societies. The other one-third are specified as lay members. Although the board has taken actions against physicians, it is not possible to judge the board's effectiveness in any precise way. According to its 2011–13 report, "Between 2011 and 2013, the Board issued an average of 380 final actions; an average of 287 of these final actions (75 percent) were serious sanctions including the revocation, surrender, or suspension of a physician's medical license, or a limitation or restriction placed on the doctor's license."[46] However, a determination of whether these actions adequately protected the citizens of New York must take into account several other facts: over these three years, 22,185 complaints were filed (a number of which were apparently not applicable to the duties of the board); in 2012, 84,474 licensed physicians were practicing in New York state; and most (71 percent) of the final actions were negotiated agreements that avoided a hearing. In the end, how well the state board performed is anyone's guess.

PUBLIC ENGAGEMENT VIA GOVERNMENT INTERVENTION

To enhance the democratic legitimacy of professional policymaking, fair representation of the public is essential. However, as the above examples show, public participation in professional policymaking is minimal, and public attention to rulemaking by the professions is scant. There are several possible reasons for this low awareness: lack of knowledge of or interest in the fields in question; a high level of public trust in the professions; the uninviting process of rulemaking; and professional isolation. One route for public involvement is through citizens' elected representatives at the state and national levels, as these examples also demonstrate.

The public, through government, has much more to say today than it did even twenty-five years ago about how medical and education funds are spent and how these services can be delivered more efficiently and less expensively. These were matters to which the professions themselves had paid little attention in the past, a choice they no longer have. To give only two examples, the 2010 Affordable Care Act has spawned dozens of private and government initiatives to reduce the costs of health care delivery.[47] These initiatives can bump up against physicians' judgments in the treatment of patients. Similarly, President Obama's stalled initiative to rate universities on the basis of cost, graduation rates, and employment after graduation is an example of an attempt to step up government intervention in higher education while stepping on the prerogatives of the academy.

More explicit and more frequent public discussions about conflicts of interest also have raised issues that private policymaking groups largely had avoided, such as physician ownership of organizations (such as physical therapy practices) to which they refer their patients, and physicians' prescribing tests in which they have a direct financial interest. Another example is the close relationship between pharmaceutical manufacturers and the physicians they pay to endorse their products. The public should be able to expect physicians to prescribe medications that will produce the best medical results, not products produced by companies that have provided something of monetary value to the physician. Some progress in this regard has been made with the passage of the Sunshine Act, a part of the Affordable Care

Act that requires more transparency in the relationship between physicians and pharmaceutical manufacturers. Since July 2013, drugs, devices, biological products, and medical supply manufacturers have been reporting to the CMS information about compensation, gifts, and other "transfers of value" to physicians. That information is now available on the CMS website.[48]

The courts, too, can help ensure that private governance serves the public interest. For example, the Supreme Court has stepped into a controversy between the North Carolina Board of Dental Examiners and the U.S. Federal Trade Commission (FTC) involving antitrust laws. The board's seven members—six dentists and one member of the general public—are appointed by the governor, and they are authorized to grant licenses for practice in the state by defining professional qualifications and testing applicants. This dentistry board ruled that clinics in the state must stop providing teeth-whitening services performed by individuals who are not licensed dentists. However, the FTC disagreed, charging that the North Carolina board was engaged in nothing more than price fixing and restraint of trade. The federal commissioners determined that applying teeth-whitening materials did not require a dental license and that the board's decision gave dentists a monopoly used for the sole purpose of setting higher prices. The board appealed to the Supreme Court of the United States. During oral arguments, Justice Breyer described the dilemma before the Court: How should the power of professionals through their state boards be protected without giving the professions the power to take advantage of their preferred position in society? He noted that he would not want the court's decision in this case to extend to other areas, say brain surgery, where he for one would want to be certain that the surgeon had the qualifications, certified by the profession, for the job. There is a large difference between teeth whitening and brain surgery, and somehow that difference has to be incorporated into public law.[49]

Special legislative commissions, too, have intervened on occasion to change policies adopted by health care professionals and their organizations. In New York state in 1984, a young person died within twenty-four hours after an emergency hospital admission; her death was attributed to improper medical care by overworked and undersupervised interns. A commission, the Bell Commission, was established to investigate the situation. In 1989 it recommended to the legislature that hospital interns should not be required to work more than eighty hours per week, half the limit set by the Accreditation Council on Graduate Medical Education (ACGME). The recommendations also included limiting interns' sequential hours on duty. The legislature enacted a law that changed the policies of a professional medical organization by imposing a public safety standard that the profession had ignored or opposed.[50]

CONCLUSION

Governance structure and policymaking processes vary among professional organizations. Awareness seems to have grown in these groups that some public or nonprofessional inputs in policymaking is important. Yet establishing and maintaining adequate channels for public participation is at best a minor consideration in their decisionmaking processes. However, nonprofessionals may have little desire to participate. Low voter turnout in elections of public officials indicates a lack of interest in public policymaking by the public in general. But the most likely limiting factors are the public's lack of the specialized knowledge required to make meaningful decisions in professional areas and professionals' reluctance to include nonprofessionals.

Members of the professional societies themselves must demand more from their societies: more transparency, more public involvement, and more accountability to a public that funds much of their professional work. A balance needs to be struck between autonomy and accountability. Eliminating conflicts of interest on one hand, and educating the public and its elected representatives on the importance of professional judgment on the other, would be a good start.

Seven

CONCLUSION: WHAT TO MAKE
OF PRIVATE GOVERNANCE?

Private governance in both concept and reality is complicated and difficult to define with precision. It can be hard to identify. Its manifestations are many. It can be closely entangled with government or separate from it. Still, this phenomenon demands to be studied systematically and more fully assessed. Nomenclature such as *public, private,* and *self-governance* needs to be sorted out and more carefully delineated. This is a world of multiple private organizations operating in twilight, making policy primarily in their own interest, and doing so with little public knowledge or participation. As long as private governance is considered to be solely a part of the market, a private right of corporations and self-governing associations, or a topic requiring high-level professional expertise beyond the competencies of the broader public, questioning private governance is off-limits.

It is difficult, in some cases nearly impossible, to draw a bright line between those private decisionmakers who operate mostly in the public interest and those for whom self-interest is the guiding light. After looking closely at three quite different areas of private policymaking—finance, food safety, and professional associations—it is apparent that private policymaking needs much more comprehensive and systematic scrutiny. Private policymakers contribute substantially to the public and have done so for years. From relieving or assisting government managers in areas from pipeline safety to the practice of medicine, private policymakers have made and continue to make major contributions in advanced democratic societies. Associations, in particular, constitute a fundamental element in a free society. Yet the argument for sustaining private governance at its current level of opacity is outweighed by the underlying propositions for sustaining open decisionmaking in a democratic society.

First, however, private governance needs to be *seen*. Making it visible is the work of scholars, specialists in think tanks, and the serious press.[1] In assessments of the causes of the near global financial meltdown of 2007–08, criticisms correctly focused on government agencies like the Securities and Exchange Commission, the Federal Reserve, the Treasury Department and its Office of the Controller of the Currency, the Federal Deposit Insurance Corporation, and others. Missing from this list of agencies was the Financial Industry Regulatory Authority (FINRA). This private organization regulates broker-dealers and could, for example, have created a stricter rule to require broker-dealers to put the interests of their clients ahead of their own.[2] FINRA's *private* regulatory zeal, oversight, and enforcement deserve closer *public* scrutiny. For the public to understand and make demands on an organization like FINRA, translators are needed, not only journalists and scholars but also policy analysts who specialize in a specific subject matter, like finance or food safety, follow closely what government agencies and private governance groups are doing, and translate this information for the interested public. However, such work needs to be done comprehensively throughout the world of private governance. Doing so would be easier if private governance were to be recognized as *public* policy. It should be its own field of study in public policy, public administration, law, and business programs.

Helping people understand the decisions and impact, both positive and negative, of private governance institutions on their lives will
be slow work for many of the reasons covered in this book. Not only
is it not yet recognized as a distinct category, but scholars know little
about it in its entirety. Lacking organizing theories beyond the normative democratic approach employed in this book, data cannot be
systematically collected and analyzed. What data are relevant? How
might the data be created? Most work on private governance (though it
is infrequently called that) is in the form of description and case studies. Both are required for a new field of study, but little else exists.

In this book we have taken some initial steps toward recognizing
private governance as a category of public policymaking and as a separate area of study. First, we defined it: private governance is authoritative policymaking by legally private groups that has a substantial impact
on a broader public. To make this definition clearer and the work of
private governance more apparent, we have examined aspects of three
areas—finance, food safety, and the professions—in some detail. The
normative standard against which to weigh private policymaking—
whether it enjoys democratic legitimacy—seems most important to
make the case that private governance is far from private but is not
held to public standards.

Democratic legitimacy is only one possible standard that might be
applied. Others include the level of expertise that private groups can
bring to bear on a problem, the effectiveness of the decisions, the
degree to which a private group's policies enhance or constrict markets, the fairness of the procedures employed in decisionmaking, and
public acceptance of the decisions made. What does private governance not do that perhaps it should? To what degree are technical
decisions actually value decisions over which the public should have a
decisive say? Under what circumstances can private policymaking be
public-serving rather than self-serving? Can private governance do a
better job of balancing benefits with costs of a new standard or regulation than government typically does?

Some of the problems associated with private governance include the serious conflicts of interest entailed in virtually all of its forms. When private interests are pitted against those of the public, the interests of those making the decisions can easily dominate unless barriers to the conflicts can be constructed. Is it possible to remove conflicts of interest in private governance?

Two oversight possibilities immediately come to mind: the courts, and for self-regulatory organizations (SROs) the government regulators with whom they work. Courts, in concert with the Federal Trade Commission and the Justice Department, can and do strike down private decisions that result in restraint of trade. Courts might be more demanding than simply employing the "best practices" of private groups in helping to determine the outcome of liability cases, but there is only so much that the courts can do. Government regulators like the SEC can closely scrutinize decisions of government-created SROs like FINRA to be sure that its decisions are primarily public-regarding.

Government agencies also can help fill in the gaps in private governance. For example, the Food Safety and Inspection Service and the Food and Drug Administration can pay more attention to the long-term, less traceable (to the retailer) aspects of food safety than private food groups are likely to do. Further, when government endorses private, consensus-based standard-setting (thus making the standards those of the government), it can and should require that those standards be publicly available and easily accessible, not sold.

Private groups themselves can do much to improve their performance. Some corporations, such the credit-rating agencies (CRAs) and many private standard-setters, should reconsider their business models. The conflicts of interest entailed in the decisions of the CRAs are inherent in their very structure: the issuers of bonds pay the CRAs for ratings, placing the CRAs in a very awkward position. Private standard-setters will never meet even the basic standard of democratic legitimacy until the standards they set are publicly available without a pay wall. Best practices should be established for private governance groups, perhaps by a hybrid group composed of private decisionmakers, government regulators, and scholars. Good government groups and think tanks, too, could hire multidisciplinary "translators" who can understand the experts in an area and can interpret technical proposals for the broader public, identify the values and public interests involved, create categories to facilitate understanding of the issues and trade-offs under consideration, and facilitate public participation.[3]

Everyone would benefit from a clearer understanding of "representation" and "public representation." Clarifying concepts is the work of scholars. Fortunately, a considerable body of work exists on the idea of representation. Unfortunately, much of this scholarship focuses on representation of the public in government, not in private or hybrid governance. To call a representative "public" without a clear demonstration of the person's connection to the public is meaningless. Can there be meaningful representation of the public outside of free and fair elections and outside of a demonstrable link between the public and the representative of that public? Further, when the link between the public and the representative becomes too loose, the chain of representation can break, as the cases of multi-stakeholder private groups (such as Extractive Industries Transparency Council), IOSCO, and the Bank for International Settlements show.[4] A person designated as a public representative should be trained, should be told how to represent the public, and should have a way to determine what the public wants. She should know exactly whom and what she is representing.

Other ways that scholars can further the work of the field of private governance is to evaluate empirical claims made in support of private governance by asking analytical questions. What is the quality of private groups' decisions? Is decisionmaking by private groups more efficient than that of government agencies? If so, what is the reason? Is there a trade-off between democracy and efficiency? How might the spirit of the Administrative Procedure Act be successfully transferred to private groups? What are the conflicts of interest confronting private governance groups, and how can they be eliminated? How do governments and private groups interact in a way that serves the public? In a pluralistic society with many different interests, what is the meaning of "serving the public"? Legal scholars can assist in sorting out the constitutional claims of private governance groups and provide alternative interpretations that would bring the public into the discussion.

Finally, scholars need to teach about private governance even though they themselves are still learning about it. Currently, students are ill-served if they are not made aware of how private groups operate and what they do. It seems to come as a surprise to many accounting students that the Financial Accounting Standards Board (FASB) is not a government agency and to students of public administration that the Governmental Accounting Standards Board (GASB) not only is private but also can dictate the actions of state and local governments. Students should know that jobs abound in this field, from third-party certification to positions within private governing organizations. Further, even when students learn about the private groups that will affect their careers, they have no larger context in which to place a FASB or GASB or in which to understand the connection between such a group and similar groups in other professions and fields. Why *should* the public have a say in the activities of private groups, students might ask? After all, they are private, aren't they? Yes they are, but they are also major players in the fields of public policy. We need to know more about them and how they operate, and devise ways to incorporate them more visibly and reasonably into public policymaking processes in systems of democratic governance.

ABBREVIATIONS

AAUP	American Association of University Professors
ABA	American Bar Association
ACCJC	Accrediting Commission for Community and Junior Colleges
ACCSC	American Commission of Career Schools and Colleges
ACGME	Accreditation Council on Graduate Medical Education
ACICS	Accrediting Council for Independent Colleges and Schools
AGA	American Gas Association
AICPA	American Institute of Certified Public Accountants
AMA	American Medical Association
AMS	Agricultural Marketing Services
ANSI	American National Standards Institute
APA	Administrative Procedure Act
ASHRAE	American Society of Heating and Air-Conditioning Engineers

ATFS	American Tree Farm System
BIS	Bank for International Settlements
BRC	British Retail Consortium Global Standards for Food Safety
CCSF	City College of San Francisco
CDFA	California Department of Food and Agriculture
CDOs	collateralized debt obligations
CEO	chief executive officer
CFPB	Consumer Financial Protection Board
CHEA	Council for Higher Education Accreditation
CMAJ	*Canadian Medical Association Journal*
CMS	Centers for Medicare and Medicaid Services
CP	Current Procedural
CPA	certified public accountant
CRA	credit-rating agency
CSA	Canadian Standards Association
CSR	corporate social responsibility
D.O.	doctor of osteopathic medicine
EMMA	Electronic Municipal Market Access
EPA	Environmental Protection Agency
ETI	Ethical Trading Initiative
EUA	European University Association
FAF	Financial Accounting Foundation
Fannie Mae	Federal National Mortgage Association
FASB	Financial Accounting Standards Board
FDA	Food and Drug Administration
FDIC	Federal Deposit Insurance Corporation
Fed	Federal Reserve
FINRA	Financial Industry Regulatory Authority
FMI	Food Marketing Institute
FOIA	Freedom of Information Act
FSB	Financial Stability Board
FSC	Forest Stewardship Council

FSMA	Food Safety Modernization Act
FSSC	Foundation for Food Safety Certification
FSVP	Foreign Supplier Verification Program
FTC	Federal Trade Commission
GAAP	generally accepted accounting principles
GAPs	good agricultural practices
GASB	Governmental Accounting Standards Board
GFSI	Global Food Safety Initiative
GlobalG.A.P.	Global Partnership for Good Agricultural Practice
GM	genetically modified
GMO	genetically modified organism
GRAS	generally regarded as safe
GRMS	global red meat standard
HACCP	Hazard Analysis Critical Control Points
HEA	Higher Education Act
HEC	Higher Education Commission
HHS	U.S. Department of Health and Human Services
HPBA	Hearth, Patio and Barbecue Association
IAF	International Accreditation Forum
IAIS	International Association of Insurance Supervisors
ICANN	Internet Corporation for Assigned Names and Numbers
ICC	International Code Council
ICE	Intercontinental Exchange
IEC	International Electrotechnical Commission
IECC	International Energy Conservation Codes
IEEE	Institute of Electrical and Electronics Engineers
IFA	International Federation of Accountants
IFS	International Food Standards
IGOs	intergovernmental organizations
IOSCO	International Organization of Securities Commissions
IPSAB	International Public Sector Accounting Standards Board
ISO	International Organization for Standardization
LCME	Liaison Committee on Medical Education

LEED	Leadership in Energy and Environmental Design
LGMA	Leafy Greens Products Handler Marketing Agreement
MLA	multilateral agreement
MSC	Marine Stewardship Council
MSRB	Municipal Securities Rulemaking Board
NACIQI	National Advisory Committee on Institutional Quality and Integrity
NAHB	National Association of Home Builders
NASAA	North American State Securities Administrators Association
NASD	National Association of Securities Dealers
NCEES	National Council of Examiners for Engineering and Surveying
NFA	National Futures Association
NFPA	National Fire Protection Association
NGO	nongovernmental organization
NIST	National Institute of Standards and Technology
NRDC	Natural Resources Defense Council
NRSRO	nationally recognized statistical rating organization
NTTAA	National Technology Transfer and Advancement Act
NYSE	New York Stock Exchange
OMB	Office of Management and Budget
OPMC	Office of Professional Medical Conduct
OPTN	Organ Procurement and Transplantation Network
OSH	occupational safety and health
OSHA	Occupational Safety and Health Administration
PAS	Publicly Available Specification
PCAOB	Public Company Accounting Oversight Board
PETA	People for the Ethical Treatment of Animals
RUC	Specialty Society Relative Value Scale Update Committee
S&P	Standard & Poor's
SDO	standards development organization
SEC	Securities and Exchange Commission

SFI	Sustainable Forestry Initiative
SGOs	self-governing organizations
SIPC	Securities Investor Protection Corporation
SPP	*Science and Public Policy*
SQF	Safe Quality Food
SQFI	Safe Quality Food Institute
SROs	self-regulatory organizations
SSRN	Social Science Research Network
TTIP	Transatlantic Trade and Investment Partnership
UL	Underwriters Laboratories
UNOS	United Network for Organ Sharing
USDA	U.S. Department of Agriculture
VQIP	Voluntary Qualified Importer Program
WASC	Western Association of Schools and Colleges
WTO	World Trade Organization

NOTES

INTRODUCTION

1. A. Lee Fritschler and Catherine E. Rudder, *Smoking and Politics: Bureaucracy Centered Policy Making*, 6th ed. (New York: Pearson, 2007).

2. Though no current, authoritative count exists, this conclusion is warranted based on the fragmentary information we have. For example, see table 1-1 in chapter 1, table 2-1 in chapter 2, and Cornelius M. Kerwin, *Rulemaking: How Government Agencies Write Law and Make Policy* (Washington, D.C.: CQ Press, 1999). This lack of data on private governance points to the urgent need for its systematic collection, based on common definitions and categories, given the importance of private governance.

3. Catherine E. Rudder, "What Is Public Policy?," in *The Future of Political Science: 100 Perspectives,* edited by Gary King, Kay Schlozman, and Norman Nie (London: Routledge Taylor & Francis, 2009): 235–37; Catherine E. Rudder, "Private Governance as Public Policy: A Paradigmatic Shift," *Journal of Politics* 70, no. 4 (October 2008): 899–913.

4. Yon Jung Choi, "Corporate Social Responsibility as World Cultural Norm? A Comprehensive Analysis of Global CSR Governance," Ph.D. dissertation in progress, George Mason University.

5. For a discussion of the public side of this distinction, see Alan McKee, *The Public Sphere: An Introduction* (Cambridge University Press, 2005).

6. See, for example, Franco Furger, "Accountability and Systems of Self-Governance: The Case of the Maritime Industry," *Law and Policy* 19 (1997): 445. The widespread use of the word *self-governance* has impact far beyond the "selves" who govern in the maritime domain. It should be noted that simply because the private sector regulates an area does not mean that that area is market-driven or subject to market imperatives, as Charles E. Lindblom has so eloquently argued in the context of the role of the corporation in the market system. See Lindblom, *The Market System: What It Is, How It Works, and What to Make of It* (Yale University Press, 2001).

7. This quote is often misattributed to the philosopher Henri Bergson.

8. A category not covered here is the growing number of private local governance organizations such as gated communities and community and condominium associations, because they do not technically fit our definition. These associations, nevertheless, may curtail the rights of citizens residing there and, in collusion with local governments, create a scheme of double taxation for residents whereby they must pay local taxes and association fees often for the same services. See Evan McKenzie, *Beyond Privatopia: Rethinking Residential Private Government* (Washington, D.C.: Urban Institute Press, 2011).

9. Giandomenico Majone, *Evidence, Argument, and Persuasion in the Policy Process* (Yale University Press, 1989).

10. Congress can and does get involved in such value choices some of the time, as the schedule for the Senate Committee on Science, Technology and Transportation shows (http://www.commerce.senate.gov/public/index .cfm?p=Hearings). This example demonstrates that even highly technical decisions can be guided by representative institutions and need not be left entirely to the "experts."

11. John Dewey, *How We Think* (Lexington, Ky.: Heath, 1910). Also see Helga Nowotny, "Democratising Expertise and Socially Robust Knowledge," *Science and Public Policy (SPP)* 30, no. 3 (June 2003): 151–56.

12. For a decidedly positive view of private governance and its history, see Edward Peter Stringham, *Private Governance: Creating Order in Economic and Social Life*, 1st ed. (Oxford University Press, 2015).

13. Michael W. Dowdle does an excellent job of assembling some leading scholars to discuss the dilemmas of public accountability in a privatized, globalized world and integrating their ideas; *Public Accountability: Designs, Di-*

lemmas and Experiences (Cambridge University Press, 2006). For more on this topic at the grassroots level, see Archon Fung and Erik Olin Wright, "Deepening Democracy: Innovations in Empowered Participatory Governance," *Politics and Society* 29 (2001): 5–41.

CHAPTER 1

1. See, for example, Robert Alan Dahl's *Polyarchy: Participation and Opposition* (Yale University Press, 1973); *On Democracy* (Yale University Press, 2001); and *A Preface to Democratic Theory* (University of Chicago Press, 1956).

2. The Federal Reserve System is composed of twelve private Reserve Banks that in addition to regulatory activities also sell services like electronic funds transfers and check-cashing to other financial institutions. For more information, see "Is the Federal Reserve a Privately-Owned Corporation?" (September 2003), Federal Reserve Bank of San Francisco, at www .frbsf.org/education/publications/doctor-econ/2003/september/private -public-corporation.

3. Ronald C. Moe, "The Emerging Federal Quasi Government: Issues of Management and Accountability," *Public Administration Review* 61, no. 3 (2001): 290–312; David L. Weimer, "The Puzzle of Private Rulemaking: Expertise, Flexibility, and Blame Avoidance in U.S. Regulation," *Public Administration Review* 66, no. 4 (2006): 569–82.

4. Whether a fourth arena institution is a private governance organization or essentially a governmental organization is a matter of degree. More work needs to be done to tackle this question. In the meantime, Kevin Kosar has suggested that, rather than using categories, a continuum could be a useful tool to distinguish among hybrid institutions. See "The Quasi Government: Hybrid Organizations with Both Government and Private Sector Legal Characteristics," Congressional Research Service, U.S. Congress, June 22, 2011 (7-5700, RL30533). In that spirit, it may be best to see hybrid and private governance institutions in the fourth and fifth arenas more broadly along a continuum according to the institutions' closeness to or independence from government, rather than place them in one category or the other. A scale based on a combination of several factors would guide where on the continuum a governance organization would fall—from hardly distinguishable from a government agency (though completely or partially private in form) to entirely self-determinative and free of any gov-

ernment control (beyond ordinary law applicable to private corporations and associations). The factors constituting the scale would include whether the organization was created by a government, whether the group is required to have operating rules and policy decisions approved by a government agency, whether its rules are used by a government, whether a government agency or court enforces its rules, whether the organization enforces agency rules, and whether it is required to report to Congress.

5. Public Law 104-113, NTTAA, followed by OMB Circular A-119, revised February 10, 1998. See ANSI Government Affairs at www.ansi.org /government_affairs/overview.aspx?menuid=6.

6. The phrase *self-governing organization* is confusing, as it can refer to private governance organizations that affect a broader public (the topic of this book) or alternatively to organizations—for instance, a local garden club—that simply makes its own rules, which have no significant impact on non-club members and hence is not a private governance group as defined here.

7. For more information on LEED, go to www.usgbc.org/leed.

8. Robert B. Toth, *Standards Activities of Organizations in the United States* (Washington, D.C.: NIST Special Publication 806, U.S. Department of Commerce, 1996), and ANSI website, www.ansi.org/about_ansi/introduction /introduction.aspx?menuid=1.

9. Ibid.

10. Tim Büthe and Walter Mattli, *The New Global Rulers: The Privatization of Regulation in the World* (Princeton University Press, 2011).

11. For example, in the international area, see A. Clair Cutler, Virginia Haufler, and Tony Porter, *Private Authority and International Affairs* (SUNY Press, 1999); Benjamin Cashore, Graeme Auld, and Deanna Newsome, "Forest Certification (Eco-Labeling) Programs and Their Policymaking Authority: Explaining Divergence among North American and European Case Studies," *Forest Policy and Economics* 5, no. 3 (2003): 225–47; Robert O. Keohane, "Global Governance and Democratic Accountability," in *Global Governance and Democratic Accountability* (Cambridge, U.K., and Malden, Mass.: Polity, 2003); Wolfgang Reinicke, *Global Public Policy: Governing without Government?* (Brookings Institution Press, 1998); David Held, *Global Transformations* (Stanford University Press, 1999); Anne Mette Kjaer, *Governance* (Cambridge, U.K.: Polity, 2004); Joseph S. Nye and John D. Donahue, *Governance in a Globalizing World* (Brookings Institution Press, 2000); James Rosenau and Ernst-Otto Czempiel, "Gover-

nance without Government: Order and Change in World Politics," in *Governance without Government* (Cambridge University Press, 1992); Maarten Hajer, "Policy without Polity? Policy Analysis and the Institutional Void," *Policy Sciences* 36 (2003): 175–95; Fabrizio Cafaggi and Andrea Renda, "Public and Private Regulation: Mapping the Labyrinth," SSRN Scholarly Paper (Rochester, N.Y.: Social Science Research Network, October 1, 2012) (http://papers.ssrn.com/abstract=2156875); Jessica F. Green, *Rethinking Private Authority: Agents and Entrepreneurs in Global Environmental Governance* (Princeton University Press, 2013); Milton L. Mueller, "Ruling the Root: Internet Governance and the Taming of Cyberspace" (MIT Press, 2002); Klaus Dingwerth, "The Democratic Legitimacy of Public-Private Rulemaking: What Can We Learn from the World Commission on Dams?," *Global Governance* 11 (2005): 65–83; Philipp Pattberg, "The Institutionalization of Private Governance: How Business and Nonprofit Organizations Agree on Transnational Rules," *Governance* 18 (2005): 589–610; David A. Wirth, "The International Organization for Standardization: Private Voluntary Standards as Swords and Shields," SSRN Scholarly Paper (Rochester, N.Y.: Social Science Research Network, February 4, 2009) (http://papers.ssrn.com/abstract =1337766); Jean-Christophe Graz and Andreas Nölke, *Transnational Private Governance and Its Limits* (London: Routledge, 2007); Sheila Seuss Kennedy, "When Is Public Private?," 2005 (sheilakennedy.net/content/view577/29). Of course, this list is only a sample of articles touching on international and global private governance.

12. Office of Management and Budget, *Federal Participation in the Development and Use of Voluntary Consensus Standards and in Conformity Assessment Activities* (Washington, D.C., 1995, rev. 1998).

13. These states have what is called a "unified bar." More information from the ABA can be found at www.americanbar.org/groups/bar_services /resources/resourcepages/unifiedbars.html.

14. For more information on the commission, go to www.jointcommission .org/about_us/about_the_joint_commission_main.aspx.

15. *Tractatus Logico-Philosophicus*, Project Gutenberg, October 27, 2010, 74 (www.gutenberg.org/ebooks/57400).

16. Michelle Ranville, "The Effectiveness of Participation in Public and Private Standard Setting," Ph.D. dissertation, George Mason University, 2014.

17. Many, but not all, private standard-setters sell their standards as a way of financing the organizations' work.

18. For an incisive exposition of the exercise of private power, see Susan Strange, *The Retreat of the State: The Diffusion of Power in the World Economy* (Cambridge University Press, 1996).

19. Giandomenico Majone, *Evidence, Argument, and Persuasion in the Policy Process* (Yale University Press, 1989).

20. Robert Michels, *Political Parties: A Sociological Study of the Oligarchical Tendencies of Modern Democracy* (New Brunswick, N.J.: Transaction Publishers, 1999).

21. Jean-Jacques Laffont and David Martimort, *The Theory of Incentives: The Principal-Agent Model* (Princeton University Press, 2009).

CHAPTER 2

1. Garfield V. Cox, "The English Building Guilds: An Experiment in Industrial Self-Government," *Journal of Political Economy* 29, no. 10 (December 1921): 777–90; and Cissie Fairchilds, "Three Views on the Guilds," *French Historical Studies* 15, no. 4 (Autumn 1988): 688–92.

2. James C. Scott, *Seeing Like a State* (Yale University Press, 1998).

3. Today the need for quality assurance in goods has grown too. The supply chain for goods has lengthened and the public's definition of quality has expanded, for example, to include environmental protection and animal and human welfare in the production of those products. Consequently, the kinds of assurances that are provided for services by third-party organizations are increasingly desired for products such as coffee, tennis shoes, and lumber.

4. Marc A. Olshan, "Standards-Making Organizations and the Rationalization of American Life," *Sociological Quarterly* 34, no. 2 (May 1993): 319.

5. Congress reversed itself in the case of the Office of Technology Assessment when it abolished that office in 1995.

6. Claire Prechtel-Kluskens, " 'Follow the Money': Tracking Revolutionary War Army Pension Payments," *Prologue Magazine* 8, no. 4 (Winter 2008), National Archives.

7. The degree of delegation from Congress to administrative agencies has been considerable, beginning with the New Deal, despite the so-called non-delegation doctrine. The Legal Information Institute of Cornell University Law School explains that the non-delegation doctrine is a "principle in administrative law that [C]ongress cannot delegate its legislative powers

to agencies. Rather, when it instructs agencies to regulate, it must give them an 'intelligible principle' on which to base their regulations." (See *Whitman* v. *American Trucking Associations, Inc.,* 531 U.S. 457 [2001].) However, the institute continues, "This standard is viewed as quite lenient, and has rarely, if ever, been used to strike down legislation" (at www.law.cornell.edu/wex/nondelegation_doctrine). In 1984 the Supreme Court, in *Chevron U.S.A., Inc.* v. *NRDC,* 467 U.S. 837, reinforced the power of agencies when it "established rules for judicial review of agency interpretations of statutes. An agency's rulemaking authority is derived through statute. Therefore, when an agency rulemaking is challenged in court, an agency's interpretation of their statutory authority is central to determining the legitimacy of the regulation" (Center for Effective Government at www.foreffectivegov.org/node/2624). This decision strengthened the hand of any agency challenged in court for overstepping its authority.

8. For an excellent discussion of some of the implications of this move, see Aaron R. Cooper, "Sidestepping *Chevron*: Reframing Agency Deference for an Era of Private Governance," *Georgetown Law Journal* 99 (2011): 1431–68. "As agencies cede regulatory authority to private actors, traditional, structural protections for core constitutional values are stripped away. And as private actors increasingly exercise interpretive authority, statutory construction will stray further from principled interpretation and fundamental rule-of-law values" (p. 1459). Cooper's solution to rely more on the courts to ensure that private actors do not stray in this manner is far from democratic and does not resolve the constitutional problem. Still, it is a practical step in the right direction.

9. Dieter Kerwer, "Watchdogs beyond Control? The Accountability of Accounting Standards Organizations," in *Organizing Transnational Accountability*, edited by Magnus Bostrom and Christina Garsten (Cheltenham, U.K.: Edward Elgar, 2008), 98–113.

10. As resources are increasingly squeezed, governments find turning to the private sector to be an attractive alternative. See Kevin Kosar, "The Quasi Government: Hybrid Organizations with Both Government and Private Sector Legal Characteristics," Congressional Research Service, U.S. Congress, June 22, 2011 (7-5700, RL30533).

11. R. Douglas Arnold, *The Logic of Congressional Action* (Yale University Press, 1992).

12. David R. Mayhew, *Congress: The Electoral Connection* (Yale University Press, 1974).

13. David Weimer, "The Puzzle of Private Rulemaking: Expertise, Flexibility, and Blame Avoidance in U.S. Regulations," *Public Administration Review* 66, no. 4 (August 2006): 569–82.

14. Figures are retrieved from a report published by the Congressional Budget Office, *Comparing the Compensation of Federal and Private-sector Employees* (January 2012) (www.cbo.gov/sites/default/files/cbofiles/attachments /01-30-FedPay.pdf).

15. As Elliott Sclar points out in his excellent monograph on the decision to contract out government work, the greater the information asymmetry between the government and the contractor, with the contractor holding the upper hand, the greater the likelihood that work will be shoddy. See Elliott D. Sclar, *You Don't Always Get What You Pay For: The Economics of Privatization* (Cornell University Press, 2001).

16. Arthur M. Okun, *Equality and Efficiency: The Big Tradeoff* (Brookings Institution Press, 1975).

17. This contention is based on the corporation's obligation to increase shareholder value.

18. This assertion assumes that an industry does not in practice control a government agency and hence cannot accomplish through the agency what it could achieve with private governance.

19. Robert E. Litan, "Why Professional Licenses Are a Barrier to Growth," *The Atlantic*, March 13, 2012 (www.theatlantic.com/business/archive/2012 /03/why-professional-licenses-are-a-barrier-to-growth/254041/).

20. Michelle Ranville, "The Effectiveness of Participation in Public and Private Standard Setting," Ph.D. dissertation, George Mason University, 2014.

21. Elinor Ostrom, *Governing the Commons: The Evolution of Institutions for Collective Action* (Cambridge University Press, 1990).

22. See, for example, Phil Weiser, "The Future of Internet Regulation," SSRN Scholarly Paper (Rochester, N.Y.: Social Science Research Network, February 16, 2009), at http://papers.ssrn.com/abstract=1344757. Weiser identifies co-regulation as "a self-regulatory body subject to public agency oversight and backstop."

23. See, for example, Gillian Brock, "Global Governance: Some Concerns about Authentic Democracy Addressed," SSRN Scholarly Paper (Rochester, N.Y.: Social Science Research Network, May 10, 2011), at http:// papers.ssrn.com/abstract=1837317; David Held, *Democracy and the Global Order* (Stanford University Press, 1995); Jerry Louis Mashaw, "Accountability and Institutional Design: Some Thoughts on the Grammar of Gov-

ernance," SSRN Scholarly Paper (Rochester, N.Y.: Social Science Research Network, 2006), at http://papers.ssrn.com/abstract=924879; Anne-Marie Slaughter, "Global Government Networks, Global Information Agencies, and Disaggregated Democracy," *SSRN eLibrary* (2004), at http://papers.ssrn.com/sol3/papers.cfm?abstract_id=283976.

24. Here is how UL describes its relationship with American governments (see http://site.ul.com/global/eng/pages/corporate/contactus/faq/general/background/):

> Manufacturers submit products to UL for testing and safety certification on a voluntary basis. There are no laws specifying that a UL Mark must be used. However, in the United States there are many municipalities that have laws, codes or regulations which require a product to be tested by a nationally recognized testing laboratory before it can be sold in their area. UL is the largest and oldest nationally recognized testing laboratory in the United States. UL does not, however, maintain a list of the jurisdictions having such regulations.
>
> If you plan to market your product nationally or internationally, it is advisable to obtain UL Listing. If a limited marketing program is anticipated, check with the municipal office having jurisdiction in the particular areas to learn the local retail ordinances or product installation requirements applicable in that area.
>
> Many companies make it their policy to obtain UL Listing not only to minimize the possibility of local non-acceptance, but also as a matter of corporate policy and commitment to minimize the possibility of risk in the use of their products.

25. UL is one of the certification companies approved by the federal Occupational Safety and Health Administration (OSHA) to implement safety testing. See www.osha.gov/dts/otpca/nrtl/index.html#nrtls.

26. Here is how OSHA defines *standard* and *national consensus standard* (see www.osha.gov/pls/oshaweb/owadisp.show_document?p_table=STANDARDS&p_id=9698):

> "Standard" means a standard which requires conditions, or the adoption or use of one or more practices, means, methods, operations, or

processes, reasonably necessary or appropriate to provide safe or healthful employment and places of employment; "National consensus standard" means any standard or modification thereof which (1) has been adopted and promulgated by a nationally recognized standards-producing organization under procedures whereby it can be determined by the Secretary of Labor or by the Assistant Secretary of Labor that persons interested and affected by the scope or provisions of the standard have reached substantial agreement on its adoption, (2) was formulated in a manner which afforded an opportunity for diverse views to be considered, and (3) has been designated as such a standard by the Secretary or the Assistant Secretary, after consultation with other appropriate Federal agencies.

27. See ANSI's description of itself at www.ansi.org/about_ansi/overview/overview.aspx?menuid=1 and http://publicaa.ansi.org/sites/apdl/Documents/News%20and%20Publications/Brochures/U.S.StandardsSystemOverview_Third_Edition.pdf. ANSI funds itself primarily through publication sales, accreditation services, and membership dues. For more information see its 2012–13 Annual Report, "Building Connections, Fostering Solutions," at www.ansi.org/about_ansi/overview/overview.aspx?menuid=1.

28. Marc A. Olshan, "Standards-Making Organizations and the Rationalization of American Life," *Sociological Quarterly* 34, no. 2 (May 1993): 327.

29. See ANSI, "Overview of the U.S. Standardization System," at www.standardsportal.org/usa_en/standards_system.aspx.

30. For relevant language in the U.S. Code, see www.law.cornell.edu/uscode/text/29/655.

31. Details on OMB Circular A-119 are at www.whitehouse.gov/omb/circulars_a119/#4.

32. Given its small size and few resources, OSHA would not be able to operate as well as it does without this private help. As the agency states on its website, "with our state partners we have approximately 2,200 inspectors responsible for the health and safety of 130 million workers, employed at more than 8 million worksites around the nation—which translates to about one compliance officer for every 59,000 workers." Further, the punishments that OSHA can impose do not make for strong enforcement authority. As OSHA explains, "The maximum penalty OSHA can assess,

regardless of the circumstances, is $7,000 for each serious violation and $70,000 for a repeated or willful violation" at www.osha.gov/OSHA_FAQs .html.

33. As budgetary pressures constrain funding for agencies, they will continue to need governance help from the private sector. For a prescient view of the government's use of private groups, see Charles L. Schultze, *Public Use of Private Interest* (Brookings Institution Press, 1977).

34. International refers to nations interacting with one another. Transnational potentially includes actors like environmental groups, professionals, and multinational corporations, among others. International bodies—also called intergovernmental organizations (IGOs)—are composed of nation states as their members, thus members are representing their states. However, transnational bodies are frequently made and composed by private members from multiple countries, not necessarily representing national interests, but representing their industry or professional interests.

35. Some pioneering scholarly research that focuses on trends in global governance includes: Dieter Kerwer, "Rules That Many Use: Standards and Global Regulation," *Governance* 18 (2005): 611–32; Wolfgang Reinicke, *Global Public Policy: Governing without Government?* (Brookings Institution Press, 1998); Joseph S. Nye and John D. Donahue, eds., *Governance in a Globalizing World* (Brookings Institution Press, 2000); Daniel W. Drezner, *All Politics Is Global: Explaining International Regulatory Regimes* (Princeton University Press, 2007); Virginia Haufler, *A Public Role for the Private Sector: Industry Self-Regulation in a Global Economy* (Washington, D.C.: Carnegie Endowment for International Peace, 2001); Peter Drahos and John Braithwaite, "The Globalisation of Regulation," *Journal of Political Philosophy* 9, no. 1 (March 2001): 103–28.

36. Jessica F. Green, *Rethinking Private Authority: Agents and Entrepreneurs in Global Environmental Governance* (Princeton University Press, 2013).

37. Multi-stakeholder groups are groups and organizations that comprise both public and private members or "stakeholders." For an explanation of a successful example of NGO-initiated global standard-setting, see Jessica F. Green, "Private Standards in the Climate Regime: The Greenhouse Gas Protocol," *Business & Politics* 12, no. 3 (September 2010): 1–37. Also see Jorge L. Contreras, "Standards and Related Intellectual Property Issues for Climate Change Technology," SSRN Scholarly Paper

(Rochester, N.Y.: Social Science Research Network, February 9, 2012), at http://papers.ssrn.com/abstract=1756283.

38. For an alternative view see, for example, Wayne Winegarden, "Competitive Standards Strengthens Oregon's Forests," *Forbes*, September 22, 2014 (www.forbes.com/sites/econostats/2014/09/22/competitive-standards -strengthens-oregons-forests/).

39. See a "Comparison of Certification Systems" from the University of Tennessee at www.forestandrange.org/Forest%20Certification/comptable .html.

40. See Mónica Brito Vieira and David Runciman, *Representation* (Cambridge, U.K.: Polity, 2008) for a useful discussion of the concept of a "chain of representation." See Anne-Marie Slaughter, *A New World Order* (Princeton University Press, 2004) for an example of the difficulty of following such a chain from the public to government officials to their global associations.

41. For a contrast between state-initiated and the rapidly expanding private-entrepreneur-initiated regulation of the environment, see Green, *Rethinking Private Authority*.

42. Mancur Olson, *The Logic of Collective Action: Public Goods and the Theory of Groups* (Harvard University Press, 1965).

43. A number of scholars have made a worthy effort in this regard. See, for example, *Debating Cosmopolitics*, edited by Daniele Archibugi (London: Verso, 2003); David Held, *Democracy and the Global Order* (Stanford University Press, 1995); Brock, "Global Governance"; David Held and Anthony G. McGrew, *Governing Globalization: Power, Authority, and Global Governance* (New York: Wiley, 2002); Achim Hurrelmann, Steffen Schneider, and Jens Steffek, eds., *Legitimacy in an Age of Global Politics* (New York: Palgrave Macmillan, 2007); Nadia Urbinati, "Can Cosmopolitical Democracy Be Democratic?," in *Debating Cosmopolitics*, 67–85; Daniele Archibugi, *The Global Commonwealth of Citizens: Toward Cosmopolitan Democracy* (Princeton University Press, 2008); Miles Kahler, "Defining Accountability Up: The Global Economic Multinationals," in *Global Governance and Public Accountability*, edited by David Held and Mathias Koenig-Archibugi (Malden, Mass.: Blackwell, 2005), 8–34.

44. Tim Büthe, "Engineering Uncontestedness? The Origins and Institutional Development of the International Electrotechnical Commis-

sion (IEC)," *Business and Politics* 12, no. 3 (September 2010): 1–62, doi:10.2202/1469-3569.1338.

45. John G. Palfrey, "The End of the Experiment: How ICANN's Foray into Global Internet Democracy Failed," SSRN Scholarly Paper (Rochester, N.Y.: Social Science Research Network, January 1, 2004), at http://papers.ssrn.com/abstract=487644. For background on ICANN, see Milton L. Mueller, *Ruling the Root: Internet Governance and the Taming of Cyberspace* (MIT Press, 2002). Note that ICANN, a nonprofit organization registered in California, operates under a contract with the U.S. Department of Commerce, a fact that certainly implies that U.S. interests underlie ICANN and reduces its transnational character. See Jack Goldsmith and Tim Wu, *Who Controls the Internet? Illusions of a Borderless World* (Oxford University Press, 2008); Jochen von Bernstorff, "Democratic Global Internet Regulation? Governance Networks, International Law and the Shadow of Hegemony," *European Law Journal* 9, no. 4 (2003): 511–26.

CHAPTER 3

1. Legitimacy and authority are coterminous for the purposes of this discussion. For more general considerations of authority, see R. P. Wolff, "The Conflict between Authority and Autonomy," in *Authority*, edited by Joseph Raz (New York University, 1990); Mark E. Warren, "Deliberative Democracy and Authority," *American Political Science Review* 90, no. 1 (March 1996): 46–60; Joseph Raz, ed., *Authority* (New York University Press, 1990). For further consideration of legitimacy at the global level, see Allen Buchanan, "Political Legitimacy and Democracy," *Ethics* 112, no. 4 (2002): 689–719; Allen Buchanan and Robert O. Keohane, "The Legitimacy of Global Governance Institutions," *Ethics and International Affairs* 20, no. 4 (2006): 405–37; A. Claire Cutler, Virginia Haufler, and Tony Porter, "The Contours and Significance of Private Authority in International Affairs," in *Private Authority and International Affairs* (State University of New York Press, 1999), 333–76; Christoph Engel, "Hybrid Governance across National Jurisdictions as a Challenge to Constitutional Law," Max Planck Institute for Research on Collective Goods Preprints (2001); Nicolas Hachez and Jan Wouters, "A Glimpse at the Democratic Legitimacy of Private Standards Assessing the Public Accountability of Global G.A.P.," *Journal of International Economic Law* 14, no. 3 (September 1,

2011): 677–710; Andreas Nolke, "Transnational Private Authority and Corporate Governance," in *New Rules for Global Markets: Public and Private Governance in the World Economy*, edited by Stefan A. Schirm (New York: Palgrave Macmillan, 2004): 155–72; and Achim Hurrelmann, Steffen Schneider, and Jens Steffek, eds., *Legitimacy in an Age of Global Politics* (New York: Palgrave Macmillan, 2007).

2. For an extensive discussion of political legitimacy as it has been understood through the ages, see Fabienne Peter, "Political Legitimacy," *The Stanford Encyclopedia of Philosophy* (Winter 2014), edited by Edward N. Zalta (http://plato.stanford.edu/archives/win2014/entries/legitimacy/).

3. For a justification and elaboration of this principle, see Archon Fung, "Infotopia: Unleashing the Democratic Power of Transparency," *Politics and Society* 41, no. 2 (June 2013): 183–212.

4. To see these principles applied in a specific case of transnational governance, see Klaus Dingwerth's "The Democratic Legitimacy of Public-Private Rulemaking: What Can We Learn from the World Commission on Dams?," in *The New Transnationalism: Transnational Governance and Democratic Legitimacy* (New York: Palgrave Macmillan, 2007). As Dingwerth points out, being able to apply these principles in practice in transnational governance is still in the early stages of development. For a thorough discussion of nation-state legitimacy, see Bruce Gilley, *The Right to Rule: How States Win and Lose Legitimacy*, 1st ed. (Columbia University Press, 2009).

5. Kathleen M. Eisenhardt, "Agency Theory: An Assessment and Review," *Academy of Management Review* 14, no. 1 (January 1, 1989): 57–74, doi:10.2307/258191.

6. For an in-depth consideration of this problem, see Paul Weissburg, "Shifting Alliances in the Accreditation of Higher Education: On the Long Term Consequences of the Delegation of Government Authority to Self-Regulatory Organizations," Ph.D. dissertation, George Mason University, 2008.

7. Jane Mansbridge, "A 'Selection Model' of Political Representation," *Journal of Political Philosophy* 17, no. 4 (December 1, 2009): 369–98, doi:10.1111/j.1467-9760.2009.00337.x.

8. Jon Elster, *Nuts and Bolts for the Social Sciences* (Cambridge University Press, 1989): 113–23.

9. Trust underpins much of Elinor Ostrom's work. See Elinor Ostrom, "Beyond Markets and States: Polycentric Governance of Complex Economic Systems," Nobel Prize Lecture, Stockholm, Sweden, December 8, 2009.

10. "Accountability and Institutional Design: Some Thoughts on the Grammar of Governance," in *Public Accountability: Designs, Dilemmas and Experiences,* edited by Michael Dowdle (Cambridge University Press, 2006), 115–56.

11. Ibid., 118.

12. Mónica Brito Vieira and David Runciman, *Representation* (Cambridge, U.K.: Polity, 2008).

13. For other examples of these kinds of entities, see Anne-Marie Slaughter, *A New World Order* (Princeton University Press, 2004).

14. See Dingwerth, "The Democratic Legitimacy of Public-Private Rulemaking."

15. Robert Alan Dahl's *Polyarchy: Participation and Opposition* (Yale University Press, 1973) is a classic example of this approach.

16. For a detailed review of the APA, see William F. Funk, Jeffrey S. Lubbers, and Charles Pou, *Federal Administrative Procedure Sourcebook* (Chicago: American Bar Association, 2008).

17. For a simple explanation of the APA and associated useful references, see the Federal Register's "A Guide to the Federal Rulemaking Process" at www.federalregister.gov. Also see A. Lee Fritschler and Catherine E. Rudder, *Smoking and Politics: Bureaucracy Centered Policy Making* (New York: Pearson, 2006).

18. Michelle Ranville, "The Effectiveness of Participation in Public and Private Standard Setting," Ph.D. dissertation, George Mason University, 2014, p. 48.

19. A possible exception to this assertion are B Corps, corporations that are explicitly dedicated to values that benefit both society and their shareholders. For more information, see www.bcorporation.net/.

20. Jedediah Purdy, "The Roberts Court v. America," *Democracy Journal* (www.democracyjournal.org/23/the-roberts-court-v-america.php).

21. This gap can be defined in a variety of ways. Here the reference is to the lack of a single authority or set of authorities (with an emphasis on the right and ability to rule) to ensure cooperation on issues, such as epidemics or global climate change, that affect the welfare of human beings across the globe.

22. Peter Grajzl and Peter Murrell offer a useful discussion of circumstances when self-regulation is preferable to government regulation ("Allocating Law-Making Powers: Self-Regulation vs. Government Regulation," *Journal of Comparative Economics* 35, no. 3 [2007]: 520–45). Much

of Elinor Ostrom's work attends to the cooperation of nonstate actors to govern themselves. See, for example, her classic volume: Elinor Ostrom, *Governing the Commons: The Evolution of Institutions for Collective Action* (Cambridge University Press, 1990).

23. Giandomenico Majone, *Evidence, Argument, and Persuasion in the Policy Process* (Yale University Press, 1989).

24. For a defense of experts in a democratic society, see Stephen Turner, "What Is the Problem with Experts?," *Social Studies of Science* 31, no. 1 (February 2001): 123–49.

25. *Richard D. Shapero, Petitioner* v. *Kentucky Bar Association*, 486 U.S. 466 (108 S. Ct. 1916, 100 L.Ed. 2nd 475).

26. *North Carolina State Board of Dental Examiners* v. *Federal Trade Commission* (2015) in which the Supreme Court, according to two law professors writing in the *Wall Street Journal*, "affirmed the FTC's position that state licensing boards controlled by 'active market participants'—those who practice the profession—are exempt from antitrust lawsuits only if they are also supervised by the state government." The scholars go on to explain that about 30 percent of the U.S. workforce must acquire an occupational license. In Florida, for example, "38 of the state's boards are required by statute to be staffed by a majority of active market participants. These boards set the terms of competition within the profession and control who is allowed to compete in the first place. This self-regulation has led to self-dealing." See Rebecca Haw Allensworth and Aaron Edlin, "Letting Dentists Feel the Bite of Competition," *Wall Street Journal*, March 9, 2015, A13. For straightforward descriptions of the two cases, see www.law.cornell.edu /supremecourt/text/486/466 and www.law.cornell.edu/supct/cert/13-534. The underlying statute is the Sherman Antitrust Law of 1890, which states that "Every contract, combination in the form of trust or otherwise, or conspiracy, in restraint of trade or commerce among the several States, or with foreign nations, is declared to be illegal" (15 U.S. Code § 1).

27. See the National Cooperative Research and Production Act of 1983. For a fuller discussion of antitrust concerns of private standards development organizations (SDOs) or consortia, see ConsortiumInfo.org at www .consortiuminfo.org/laws/#2.

28. "Understanding the Rate-Fixing Inquiry," Business Day DealBook, *New York Times,* updated July 28, 2014 (www.nytimes.com/interactive /2012/07/16/business/dealbook/20120716-libor-interactive.html).

29. See Majone, *Evidence, Argument, and Persuasion in the Policy Process,* for an enlightening discussion of this distinction.

CHAPTER 4

1. The board of trustees of the FAF is nominated in part by a group of interested constituent organizations such as the American Accounting Association, the American Institute of Certified Public Accountants, the CFA Institute, Financial Executives International, the Government Finance Officers Association, the Institute of Management Accountants, the National Association of State Auditors, Comptrollers and Treasurers, and the Securities Industry Association, among others. The FAF also oversees the private Governmental Accounting Standards Board (GASB), the Financial Accounting Standards Advisory Council, the Governmental Accounting Standards Advisory Council, and a new organization, the Private Company Council, which works with FASB on determining whether to alter the generally accepted accounting principles (GAAP). For more information, go to www.accountingfoundation.org.

2. As FASB explains on its website, "Since 1973, the Financial Accounting Standards Board (FASB) has been the designated organization in the private sector for establishing standards of financial accounting that govern the preparation of financial reports by nongovernmental entities. Those standards are officially recognized as authoritative by the Securities and Exchange Commission (SEC) (Financial Reporting Release No. 1, Section 101, and reaffirmed in its April 2003 Policy Statement) and the American Institute of Certified Public Accountants (Rule 203, Rules of Professional Conduct, as amended May 1973 and May 1979)" (http://www.fasb .org/jsp/FASB/Page/SectionPage&cid=1176154526495).

3. NYSE-EuroNext, owned by Atlanta-based Intercontinental Exchange.

4. Through the NASD, another self-regulatory organization, securities dealers regulated themselves with the imprimatur of statute and the SEC since its founding in the wake of the Great Depression. The NASD was merged into FINRA upon its creation in 2007.

5. See FINRA, "Enforcement," at www.Finra.org/Industry/Enforcement/.

6. Established in 1887, the AICPA counts 400,000 members in 145 countries. It is the major professional association in the United States for certified public accountants (CPAs). It develops and grades the Uniform

CPA Examination and certifies CPAs working in specific fields, such as financial planning. All members are to abide by the AICPA code of conduct, the ethical standards of the profession. The organization itself proclaims that it has a history of "serving the public interest" (www.aicpa.org). The limiting of its authority can be understood in the context of FASB's statement: "The SEC has statutory authority to establish financial accounting and reporting standards for publicly held companies under the Securities Exchange Act of 1934. Throughout its history, however, the Commission's policy has been to rely on the private sector for this function *to the extent that the private sector demonstrates ability to fulfill the responsibility in the public interest*" (www.fasb.org, emphasis added). The authority to set and oversee compliance with accounting rules has stayed in the private sector but has shifted away from the AICPA to FASB and PCAOB.

7. For more information on NASAA, go to www.nasaa.org.

8. GASB board members typically hail from the governments (treasurers, budget office heads, and others) that must follow GASB rules. This fact potentially creates a conflict of interest between wanting high standards and having to meet those standards. A further complication is that the GASB board has been slow to recognize problems that could possibly have been prevented, such as the practice of underfunding pension and other retirement benefit funds.

9. Although the federal government is not subject to GASB rules, it, too, receives an unsolicited rating on the quality of its debt from the private, for-profit credit raters. Sovereign debt ratings, like those for corporate securities, affect the cost of capital or interest rate level that a country must offer in order to attract a sufficient number of investors.

10. For a report from an academic conference on underfunded pensions and their future impact, see "Underfunded Pensions: Tackling an 'Invisible' Crisis,'" *Knowledge@Wharton*, January 26, 2015, at http://knowledge.wharton.upenn.edu/article/underfunded-pensions-tackling-an-invisible-crisis/. For data on underfunded public pensions, see http://publicplansdata.org/quick-facts/national/. On the size of the total liability, see Mary Williams Walsh, "Bad Math and a Coming Public Pension Crisis," *New York Times*, July 8, 2015.

11. See SIPC, "Message from the Board of Directors," at www.sipc.org. Note that this government-mandated participation in a private governance group is not limited to the financial field. See chapter 5's description

of marketing orders requiring agricultural producers and handlers to join and pay dues to self-regulating commodity groups overseen by the USDA. Similarly, large companies with defined benefit pensions must contribute to the Pension Benefit Guarantee Corporation to ensure that retirees receive at least a portion of their promised pensions should a company fail.

12. According to the rubric outlined earlier in the book, NASAA is a fifth-arena organization and the PCAOB falls into the fourth arena, but the question "public or private?" points to the twilight in which such organizations exist and the fragile link between them and the public.

13. This description comes from www.bis.org/about/history.htm.

14. Adam LeBor, *Tower of Basel: The Inside Story of the Central Bankers' Secret Bank* (PublicAffairs, 2013).

15. See International Organization of Securities Commissions at www.iosco.org/about/.

16. See Financial Stability Board at www.financialstabilityboard.org/about/overview.htm.

17. Viktoria Dendrinou, "Big Banks Face New Capital Requirement," *Wall Street Journal,* November 10, 2014, C3. Domestically, government regulators must decide which banks are to be treated as systemically important and other weighty matters.

18. Here is the IAIS's description of itself: "Established in 1994, the IAIS represents insurance regulators and supervisors of more than 200 jurisdictions in nearly 140 countries, constituting 97% of the world's insurance premiums. It also has more than 130 observers. Its objectives are to: Promote effective and globally consistent supervision of the insurance industry in order to develop and maintain fair, safe and stable insurance markets for the benefit and protection of policyholders; and to [c]ontribute to global financial stability" (www.iaisweb.org).

19. James Madison's *Federalist* No. 10 clearly states this concern as a justification for the decisions made at the Constitutional Convention in 1787.

20. The distancing on the last two items is typical in developed economies where parliaments cannot interfere with decisions of the central banks. Representative assemblies typically set the rules that guide the banks but cannot overrule their decisions.

21. For an explanation, see Evan Schnidman, "Why the Federal Reserve is Dodd-Frank's Big Winner, *Harvard Business Law Review* 1

(2011) at www.hblr.org/2011/06/why-the-federal-reserve-is-dodd-franks
-big-winner/.

22. See "Structure and Functions of the Federal Reserve System" at
www.federalreserveeducation.org/about-the-fed/structure-and-functions/.

23. A movement is afoot to alter the way the presidents of the regional
banks are selected. A coalition of community groups and labor unions
has called the current process "secretive, undemocratic and dominated by
banks and large corporations." Ady Barkan, a lawyer with the advocacy
group Center for Popular Democracy, pointed to a key reason for substantial public involvement in the selection of presidents of the regional reserve
banks (and by implication in the selection of the boards of private governance groups more broadly): "The Federal Reserve has huge influence over
the number of people who have jobs, over our wages, over the number of
hours *that we get to work, and yet we don't have discussion and engagement
over what* Fed policy should be. . . . More voices need to be heard." Binya-
min Appelbaum, "Coalition Calls for Public Input as Federal Reserve Selects New Top Officials," *New York Times*, November 11, 2014, B3.

24. Jerry Mashaw, "Accountability and Institutional Design: Some
Thoughts on the Grammar of Governance," in *Public Accountability: Designs,
Dilemmas and Experiences*, edited by Michael Dowdle (Cambridge Univer-
sity Press, 2006), 115–56.

25. See Financial Crisis Inquiry Commission, Financial Crisis Inquiry
Report Authorized Report, Final Report of the National Commission on
the Causes of the Financial and Economic Crisis in the United States
(New York: Public Affairs, 2011); and Alan S. Blinder, *After the Music
Stopped: The Financial Crisis, the Response, and the Work Ahead*, 1st ed. (New
York: Penguin Press, 2013). Blinder discusses the unreliability of self-
regulation, among many other matters.

26. Richard L. Stone and Michael A. Perino, "Not Just a Private Club:
Self Regulatory Organizations as State Actors When Enforcing Federal
Law," *Columbia Business Law Review 1995*, no. 2 (1995): 453.

27. For a list of securities-related SROs, go to www.sec.gov/rules/sro
.shtml.

28. These fees include assessments on municipal securities that are issued; annual and initial charges to dealers; and transaction and technology
fees. Municipal advisors, as well, are assessed based on the size of securities involved. MSRB also sells subscriptions to its proprietary data. Fines
assessed on dealers, brokers, firms, and others for violations of MSRB or

federal rules are shared with FINRA, as collector, and the SEC, which approves the application of such penalties.

29. Lynn Hume, "SEC Chair's Salary Far Below Group Execs Representing Firms, Individuals Overseen," *Bond Buyer*, September 3, 2013, at www.bondbuyer.com/issues/122_170/sec-chairs-salary-far-below-firm-executives-overseen-regulated-1055210-1.html. The salary set for the PCAOB chair in 2011 was close to $670,000 per year, while the other four board members received almost $550,000 that year. See www.reuters.com/article/2012/01/10/us-sec-pcaob-budget-idUSTRE8090TH20120110.

30. Michael Smallberg, "Dangerous Liaisons: Revolving Door at SEC Creates Risk of Regulatory Capture," *Project on Government Oversight* (February 11, 2013), at www.pogo.org/our-work/reports/sec-revolving-door.html.

31. As the noted economist Robert E. Litan observed, "One has a hard time thinking . . . of the regulation of any other sector of the economy whose failure contributed to an economic calamity of the magnitude of the 2007–08 financial crisis and subsequent recession." See "The Political Economy of Financial Regulation after the Crisis" in *Rethinking the Financial Crisis*, edited by Alan S. Blinder, Andrew W. Lo, and Robert M. Solow (New York: Russell Sage Foundation, 2012), 269–302.

32. FINRA did not exist in 2005, but its predecessors, the National Association of Securities Dealers and NYSE Regulation, did.

33. One exception to this assertion is that Lehman Brothers was allowed to fail. It could be said that the public was not protected either. The conclusion people draw depends on their perspectives. Compare, for example, Dean Baker's critical assessment of January 28, 2013, for the Center for Economic and Policy Research (www.cepr.net/index.php/op-eds-&-columns/op-eds-&-columns/timothy-geithner-saved-wall-street-not-the-economy) with Treasury Secretary Timothy Geithner's assessment in *Stress Test: Reflections on Financial Crises* (New York: Random House, 2014). The billions of dollars in fines that the SEC has imposed on investment banks are another exception, though the banks for the most part have refused to admit guilt and continue to thrive, as do the individuals who were most responsible for the fiasco.

34. For a history of FINRA, see www.sechistorical.org/museum/galleries/sro/sro06g.php.

35. For more information about the Financial Industry Regulatory Authority, see www.finra.org.

36. According to *Bloomberg*, "Dark pools have a scary name, and to critics they're scary places: private stock markets housed inside some of Wall Street's biggest banks. Created to let big investors swap large blocks of shares in secret, they've expanded to become a significant part of daily stock trading. More shares now change hands in dark pools than on the New York Stock Exchange. Dark pools have helped bring down trading costs. But whether markets as a whole suffer when too much trading information is private is something regulators around the world are trying to figure out—along with whether some dark pools have been taking advantage of the darkness to favor some customers over others." Sam Mamudi, "Dark Pools: Private Stock Trading vs. Public Exchanges," *Bloomberg*, October 8, 2014 (www.bloombergview.com/quicktake/dark-pools).

37. Investopedia defines a derivative as "A security whose price is dependent upon or derived from one or more underlying assets. The derivative itself is merely a contract between two or more parties. Its value is determined by fluctuations in the underlying asset. The most common underlying assets include stocks, bonds, commodities, currencies, interest rates and market indexes. Most derivatives are characterized by high leverage [or borrowed capital]" (www.investopedia.com/terms/d/derivative.asp). Gary Gensler tried during his chairmanship (2009–14) of the U.S. Commodities Futures Trading Commission to strengthen government oversight of this area but to little avail. The U.S. public exchanges for commodities that deal in derivatives to a large degree (CME Group, Chicago Board of Trade, New York Mercantile Exchange, and COMEX) are separate SROs, though they try to harmonize their rules with each other and with FINRA, which also is contracted in many cases to enforce such groups' rules.

38. At http://finra.complinet.com/en/display/display_main.html?rbid=2403&element_id=4711.

39. See, for example, Stephen Labaton, "S.E.C. Concedes Oversight Flaws Fueled Collapse," *New York Times*, September 27, 2008, Business sec.

40. Susan Antilla, "In Push for Change, Finra Is Opposed by the Firms It Regulates," *New York Times*, January 27, 2015.

41. Timothy J. Fogarty, Mohammed E. A. Hussein, and J. Edward Ketz, "Political Aspects of Financial Accounting Standard Setting in the USA," *Accounting, Auditing and Accountability Journal* 7 (1994): 24–46.

42. Although CRA stands for credit-rating agency, it is a highly misleading term; CRAs are not part of the government as the word "agency" typically implies.

43. As the Financial Crisis Inquiry Commission stated on page xxv of its final report, "*We conclude the failures of credit rating agencies were essential cogs in the wheel of financial destruction.* The three credit-rating agencies were key enablers of the financial meltdown. The mortgage-related securities at the heart of the crisis could not have been marketed and sold without their seal of approval. Investors relied on them, often blindly. In some cases, they were obligated to use them, or regulatory capital standards were hinged on them. This crisis could not have happened without the rating agencies. Their ratings helped the market soar and their downgrades through 2007 and 2008 wreaked havoc across markets and firms" [emphasis in original]. See *Financial Crisis Inquiry Report: Final Report of the National Commission on the Causes of the Financial and Economic Crisis in the United States*, Submitted by the Financial Crisis Inquiry Commission, Pursuant to Public Law 111-21 (January 2011), U.S. Government Printing Office.

44. Gatekeepers are to keep financial markets honest, provide accurate information on the solidity of institutions and financial instruments to investors, and engender trust that makes financial markets possible. See Claudia Gabbioneta, Rajshree Prakash, and Royston Greenwood, "Sustained Corporate Corruption and Processes of Institutional Ascription within Professional Networks," *Journal of Professions and Organization* 1, no. 1 (March 1, 2014): 16–32, doi:10.1093/jpo/jot002. Such gatekeepers including financial analysts, auditors and accountants, lawyers, investment banks, and rating agencies serve as reputational intermediaries between the public and financial institutions. See John C. Coffee, "A Theory of Corporate Scandals: Why the USA and Europe Differ," *Oxford Review of Economic Policy* 21, no. 2 (June 20, 2005): 198–211, doi:10.1093/oxrep/gri012. These gatekeepers have failed miserably in the twenty-first century. See John C. Coffee Jr., *Gatekeepers: The Professions and Corporate Governance* (Oxford University Press, 2006).

45. A capital requirement is the amount of liquidity or cash an institution needs to ride out operating losses while honoring withdrawals. The purpose of capital requirements is to ensure that the institution does not collapse even in times of duress.

46. "The Enduring Ratings Racket: Regulators Sue the Credit Raters Whose Profit Margins They Guarantee," *Wall Street Journal*, December 6, 2013, Opinion sec.; Ben Protess, "A $1.37 Billion Reckoning over Crisis-Era Misdeeds," *New York Times*, February 4, 2015.

47. Ben Protess and Nathaniel Popper, "S. & P. Deal Leaves Future Unclear for Ratings," *New York Times*, February 4, 2013.

48. According to the 2011 Financial Crisis Inquiry Report of the National Commission, 73 percent of mortgage-backed securities that were rated AAA in 2006 were massively downgraded in 2008 and were rated "junk" by 2010—a little late, to say the least, to protect investors or the larger public. Also see Patrick Bolton, Xavier Freixas, and Joel Shapiro, "The Credit Ratings Game," *Journal of Finance* 67, no. 1 (February 1, 2012): 85–111; Frank Partnoy, "How and Why Credit Rating Agencies Are Not Like Other Gatekeepers," SSRN Scholarly Paper (Rochester, N.Y.: Social Science Research Network, May 4, 2006) (http://papers.ssrn.com/abstract =900257); and Pavlos Maris, "The Regulation of Credit Rating Agencies in the U.S. and Europe: Historical Analysis and Thoughts on the Road Ahead," SSRN Scholarly Paper (Rochester, N.Y.: Social Science Research Network, July 15, 2009), at http://papers.ssrn.com/abstract=1434504.

49. Partnoy, "How and Why Credit Rating Agencies Are Not Like Other Gatekeepers," 11.

50. See ibid. for a lengthier exposition of these three reasons.

51. For more background on NRSROs, see Gary Shorter and Michael V. Seitzinger, "Credit Rating Agencies and Their Regulation" (Congressional Research Service, U.S. Congress, September 3, 2009).

52. Matt Robinson, Jody Shenn, and Sarah Mulholland, "Ratings Shopping Revived in Asset-Backed Rebound: Credit Markets," *BloombergBusiness*, March 14, 2013.

53. Council on Foreign Relations, "The Credit Rating Controversy," at www.cfr.org/financial-crises/credit-rating-controversy/p22328.

54. Sam Hananel, "Investors Face More Restrictions on Securities Class Action Cases," *Claims Journal*, June 25, 2014 (www.claimsjournal.com/news /national/2014/06/25/250760.htm).

55. For an even-handed approach to the U.S. regulatory system and its failures, see Cary Coglianese, ed., *Regulatory Breakdown: The Crisis of Confidence in U.S. Regulation* (University of Pennsylvania Press, 2012).

CHAPTER 5

1. The Federal Food and Drugs Act of 1906 (34 Stat. 768 (1906)) initiated major legislation in this area. Attributes of food that have potential

influence on health and life fall into the category "food safety," whereas all other attributes (including "food safety") are in the category "food quality." Therefore food quality is a broader term. Spencer Henson, "The Role of Public and Private Standards in Regulating International Food Markets," *Journal of International Agricultural Trade and Development* 4, no. 1 (2008): 63.

2. Spencer Henson and Thomas Reardon, "Private Agri-food Standards: Implications for Food Policy and the Agri-food System," *Food Policy* 30, no. 3 (June 2005): 244.

3. At least fifteen federal agencies are involved in regulating food safety and quality, including the Food and Drug Administration (FDA), the U.S. Department of Agriculture (USDA), the Department of Health and Human Services (HHS), and the Environmental Protection Agency (EPA). Missions, rules, and regulating methods vary among the agencies. See Ron Nixon, "Obama Proposes Single Overseer for Food Safety," *New York Times*, February 20, 2015.

4. Cecilia Carlsson and Helena Johansson, "Private Standards: Leveling the Playing Field for Global Competition in the Food Supply Chain?," *AgriFood Economic Center Report* (Lund University School of Economics and Management, 2013), at http://lup.lub.lu.se/record/4194423.

5. See Centers for Disease Control and Prevention, "Estimates of Foodborne Illnesses," at http://cdc.gov/foodborneburden/; and Ronald White, "The Need for Speed," Center for Effective Government (blog), October 15, 2014, at http://foreffectivegov.org/blog/need-speed-15-billion -cost-foodborne-illness-underscores-urgent-fda-action.

6. The Codex Alimentarius Commission was established jointly in 1963 by two international organizations, the Food and Agriculture Organization of the United Nations and the World Trade Organization in order to coordinate global food safety standards. See "Codex Alimentarius: International Food Standards," at www.codexalimentarius.org/; see also Doris Fuchs and Agni Kalfagianni, "The Causes and Consequences of Private Food Governance," *Business and Politics* 12, no. 3 (2010): 11. The WTO Sanitary and Phytosanitary Measures (SPS agreement) can be only applied to products traded, not to production methods. Carlsson and Johansson, "Private Standards," 7.

7. Details on the FSMA can be found on the FDA's website at www.fda .gov/Food/GuidanceRegulation/FSMA/default.htm.

8. The FSMA requires the FDA to establish "a voluntary, user-fee funded voluntary qualified importer program (VQIP)" so that qualified importers can expedite their imports to the United States. To meet the requirements, importers should achieve certification by an accredited third party. Through bilateral arrangements and agreements with foreign governments, some foreign food production facilities are inspected by FDA's foreign post staff, such as those in China, India, and some European and Latin American countries. However, given the large volume of food imports from all over the world, staff and resources are seriously short of fulfilling the missions. In fact, less than 2 percent of food imports are inspected by FDA staff. See Ron Nixon, "Obama Proposes Single Overseer for Food Safety," *New York Times*, February 20, 2015. See also FDA, "Food Safety Modernization Act: Frequently Asked Questions," at www.fda.gov/Food /GuidanceRegulation/FSMA/ucm247559.htm.

9. John Humphrey, "Food Safety, Private Standards Schemes and Trade: The Implications of the FDA Food Safety Modernization Act," *IDS Working Papers* 403 (2012): 8; FDA, "Full Text of the Food Safety Modernization Act (FSMA), at www.fda.gov/food/guidanceregulation/fsma/ucm247548 .htm#SEC305; and FDA, "Report to Congress on the FDA Foreign Offices," at www.fda.gov/Food/GuidanceRegulation/FSMA/ucm291803.htm.

10. Monopsony refers to a situation in which only one buyer purchases from many suppliers in a certain market. Conversely, oligopsony involves a small number of buyers purchasing from many suppliers. In these circumstances, a limited number of buyers would hold the power to control the market and price.

11. USDA data from USDA, "Global Food Markets," at www.ers.usda .gov/topics/international-markets-trade/global-food-markets/global-food -industry.aspx.

12. See U.S. Department of Agriculture, "Retailing and Wholesaling," at www.ers.usda.gov/topics/food-markets-prices/retailing-wholesaling/retail -trends.aspx#.UzxUSvl5O8A.

13. Henson, "The Role of Public and Private Standards in Regulating International Food Markets," 66.

14. Carlsson and Johansson, "Private Standards," 11.

15. Henson and Reardon, "Private Agri-food Standards," 243; Carlsson and Johansson, "Private Standards," 14.

16. There have been tensions between the United States and the European Union regarding the banning of GMO products. The U.S. govern-

ment and industry have insisted that the restriction by the EU of GMO products is an unfair trade barrier against WTO rules. See James Kenter, "U.S. Calls on Europe to Ease Limits on Gene-Altered Food," *New York Times*, June 17, 2014. Also see Martin Livermore, "Politically Modified," *Wall Street Journal*, November 7, 2007 (http://online.wsj.com/articles /SB119438764547884391).

17. Reported by USDA, cited from Drake Bennette, "Inside Monsanto, America's Third-Most-Hated Company," *Bloomberg Business Week*, July 13, 2014.

18. Henson and Reardon, "Private Agri-food Standards," 246; Henson, "The Role of Public and Private Standards in Regulating International Food Markets," 66. It is noted that impoverished people may well be concerned about GMOs in their food but cannot afford to purchase food not adulterated by GMOs; further, weak governments in less- and least-developed countries where the poorest people live are frequently unable or unwilling to control the presence of GMOs in their food supplies. At the same time, GMOs promise another green revolution that could greatly reduce world hunger.

19. Henson and Reardon, "Private Agri-food Standards," 243.

20. Henson explains the usefulness of private food standards: "Where public standards are well-developed and afford a high level of food safety and/or quality, there may still be an incentive to implement private standards, for example as a means to manage liability, limit exposure to potential regulatory action and/or pre-empt future regulatory developments. . . . Standards act to reduce the transaction costs and risks associated with procurement, especially where high levels of oversight are required in order to ensure that food safety and quality attributes are delivered." Henson, "The Role of Public and Private Standards in Regulating International Food Markets," 69.

21. Henson and Reardon, "Private Agri-food Standards," 244–45.

22. See ibid.; Henson, "The Role of Public and Private Standards in Regulating International Food Markets," 64; Doris Fuchs, Agni Kalfagianni, and Tetty Havinga, "Actors in Private Food Governance: The Legitimacy of Retail Standards and Multistakeholder Initiatives with Civil Society Participation," *Agriculture and Human Values* 28 (September 2011): 354.

23. Henson, "The Role of Public and Private Standards in Regulating International Food Markets," 65; Carlsson and Johansson, "Private Standards," 19.

24. The Safe Quality Food (SQF) standard is the most widely accepted private "good manufacturing practice" certification in the United States.

25. Humphrey, "Food Safety, Private Standards Schemes and Trade," 32.

26. "Hormone beef, GMOs, and chlorinated chicken" are currently allowed in the United States and banned in Europe. There have been heated debates over these controversial foods, and negotiators have been unable to reach compromises in dealing with them. See Claudia Schmucker, "Uncompromised Food and Safety Standards: Why TTIP's Regulatory Harmonization Will Not Equal Regulatory Erosion," Atlantic-Community .org, November 10, 2014 (https://dgap.org/en/think-tank/publications /further-publications/uncompromised-food-and-safety-standards). There was a similar debate over the use of certain pesticides such as atrazine (banned in Europe but not in the United States) during the TTIP discussion. Read Danny Hakim, "A Pesticide Banned, or Not, Underscores Trans-Atlantic Trade Sensitivities," *New York Times*, February 23, 2015.

27. "McDonald's Works to Maintain Sustainability," McDonald's news release, December 21, 2011 (http://news.mcdonalds.com/press-releases /mcdonald-s-works-to-mainstream-sustainability-nyse-mcd-0835223).

28. See McDonald's description of its food safety system at www .mcdonalds.ca/ca/en/food/making_informed_choices/food_safety.html.

29. Sara Fister Gale, "McDonald's USA: A Golden Arch of Supply Chain Food Safety," *Food Safety Magazine*, February/March 2006 (www .foodsafetymagazine.com/magazine-archive1/februarymarch-2006 /mcdonalds-usa-a-golden-arch-of-supply-chain-food-safety/).

30. Ibid.

31. Food Safety News, "A Food Safety 'Belt and Suspenders' System May be Emerging in China," June 30, 2014 (www.foodsafetynews.com/2014 /06/a-food-safety-belt-suspenders-system-may-be-emerging-in-china/#.VCL _PfldU8c).

32. To review problems in coordinating individual food safety and quality systems (especially traceability systems) and governmental regulations, and possible conflicts of interest, see Michael Ollinger and Danna Moore, "The Interplay of Regulation and Market Incentives in Providing Food Safety," *Economic Research Report* 75 (U.S. Department of Agriculture, Economic Research Service, July 2009).

33. Maki Hatanaka and others, "Third-Party Certification in the Global Agrifood System" *Food Policy* 30 (June 2005): 357; L. Manning and R. N.

Baines, "Effective Management of Food Safety and Quality," *British Food Journal* 106, no. 8 (2004): 599.

34. Those suppliers that wish to be certified have to pay for the certification, and third-party certifiers pay for their accreditation.

35. The Food and Agriculture Organization (FAO) of the United Nations certifies SQF as a Good Manufacturing Practice, and the GlobalG.A.P. as a Good Agricultural Practice. See FAO Report, *Private Standards in the United States and European Union Markets: Implications for Developing Countries* (New York: Food and Agriculture Organization of the United Nations, 2007) at www.fao.org/docrep/010/a1245e/a1245e00.HTM.

36. The U.S. members of the FMI are "nearly 40,000 retail food stores and 25,000 pharmacies, representing a combined annual sales volume of almost $770 billion," according to its official website: www.fmi.org/about-us. See also Fuchs and others, "Actors in Private Food Governance," 355.

37. Eighty-seven are American, two Canadian, and one Japanese. The other two are the president of the FMI and a staff coordinator of the FMI. See Food Marketing Institute at www.fmi.org/forms/committee/Committee FormPublic/viewExecCommittee?id=2BE4000004FD.

38. Henson, "The Role of Public and Private Standards in Regulating International Food Markets," 71; Fuchs and others, "Actors in Private Food Governance" 355; United Nations, Food and Agriculture Organization, *Private Standards in the United States and European Union Markets: Implications for Developing Countries* (2007).

39. Fuchs and others, "Actors in Private Food Governance," 361.

40. For more information about the SQFI, see www.sqfi.com/forms /committee/CommitteeFormPublic/view?id=88A2000001CF&year; www .sqfi.com/about-sqf/; and www.sqfi.com/uploadFiles/18BDF00000186.file name.Committee_Bios.pdf.

41. See SQFI, *Criteria for SQF Certification Bodies*, 7th ed. (July 2012), at www.sqfi.com/wp-content/uploads/Criteria-for-Certification-Bodies-7-24 -12.pdf .

42. The GFSI was established by a group of global retailers in 2000 with the purpose of achieving harmonization among globally accepted food standards. The figure 75–99 percent came from a survey conducted in 2006. Henson, "The Role of Public and Private Standards in Regulating International Food Markets"; Fuchs and others, "Actors in Private Food Governance."

43. The GFSI website (www.mygfsi.com/about-gfsi.html); Hatanaka and others, "Third-Party Certification in the Global Agrifood System"; L. Manning and R. N. Baines, "Effective Management of Food Safety and Quality," *British Food Journal* 106, no. 8 (2004): 599.

44. Carlsson and Johansson, "Private Standards," 26.

45. See GlobalG.A.P. website at www.globalgap.org/uk_en/who-we-are /members/.

46. Fuchs and others, "Actors in Private Food Governance," 361; Global Food Safety Initiative (www.mygfsi.com/about-us/about-gfsi/structure-and -governance.html).

47. Although the GFSI board structure was revised in 2008 to be more inclusive, retailers still constitute the majority of the board. Fuchs and others, "Actors in Private Food Governance," 360; GFSI Report, *An Overview of GFSI and Accreditation Certification,* March 2011 (www.mygfsi.com /gfsifiles/Overview_of_GFSI_and_Accredited_Certification.pdf).

48. GFSI, *GFSI Guidance Document*, 6th ed. (Issy-les-Moulineaux, France, 2011), 11 (www.mygfsi.com/gfsifiles/gfsi_guidance/GFSI_Guidance _Document.pdf).

49. Ibid., 66.

50. Good agricultural practices (GAPs) generally refer to those widely accepted production and processing practices of agricultural products as safe and sound.

51. EurepGap was established by the Euro-Retailer Produce Working Group (EUREP) in 1997 and was renamed GlobalG.A.P. in 2007. GlobalG.A.P. has set voluntary standards for the certification of agricultural products that are produced and traded globally. See Fuchs and Kalfagianni, "The Causes and Consequences of Private Food Governance," 5. Also refer to the GlobalG.A.P. website (www.globalgap.org/uk_en/who-we-are /history/Timeline/).

52. Nicolas Hachez and Jan Wouters, "Democratic Legitimacy as Public Accountability: The Case of Global G.A.P.," Working Paper 60, Lauven Center for Global Governance Studies, 2011, 15.

53. For more on GlobalG.A.P.'s makeup and committees, see "Who We Are" at www.globalgap.org/uk_en/who-we-are/governance/board/.

54. For details on GlobalG.A.P. certification, see "What We Do" at www .globalgap.org/uk_en/what-we-do/the-gg-system/certification/.

55. Klaus Dingwerth, *The New Transnationalism: Transnational Governance and Democratic Legitimacy* (New York: Palgrave Macmillan, 2007).

56. Henson and Reardon, "Private Agri-food Standards," 252.

57. Examples of these initiatives are Social Accountability 8000 (SA8000), the Ethical Trading Initiative (ETI), and the Marine Stewardship Council (MSC). Hatanaka and others, "Third-Party Certification in the Global Agrifood System," 365. More information about these examples can be found at www.sa-intl.org/ (Social Accountability International); www.ethicaltrade.org/ (Ethical Trading Initiative (ETI)); and www.msc .org/ (Marine Stewardship Council).

58. Carlsson and Johansson, "Private Standards," 18.

59. Hatanaka and others, "Third-Party Certification in the Global Agrifood System," 355, explain that the role of third-party certifiers is "assessing, evaluating, and certifying safety and quality claims based on a particular set of standards and compliance methods."

60. Tetty Havinga, "Private Regulation of Food Safety by Supermarkets," *Law and Policy* 28, no. 4 (October 2006): 526, 527.

61. In the case of the FASB, the legislation in question was the Sarbanes-Oxley Act of 2002.

62. Fuchs and others, "Actors in Private Food Governance," 356.

63. Ibid., 353.

64. Henson and Reardon, "Private Agri-food Standards," 249; Fuchs and others, "Actors in Private Food Governance," 354.

65. Henson and Reardon, "Private Agri-food Standards," 251.

66. Food and Drug Administration, "Foreign Supplier Verification Programs for Importers of Food for Humans and Animals," proposed rules, July 29, 2013 (www.fda.gov/downloads/Food/GuidanceRegulation /FSMA/UCM362670.pdf).

67. Humphrey, "Food Safety, Private Standards Schemes and Trade," 7.

68. In the case of marketing agreements, whether to participate and comply with the standards set by marketing orders is voluntary for the signatories. See Robert C. Keeney, *Marketing Orders and Agreements for Fruits, Vegetables, and Specialty Crops* (USDA Agricultural Marketing Service) at www.ams.usda.gov/AMSv1.0/getfile?dDocName=STELPRDC5065608.

69. USDA, Agricultural Marketing Service (www.ams.usda.gov/AMSv1 .0/FVMarketingOrderLandingPage).

70. "Marketing Orders, Agreements Perform Different Functions," *Fruit Growers News*, January 2011 (http://fruitgrowersnews.com/index.php /50th-anniversary/entry/marketing-orders-agreements-perform-different -functions).

71. USDA, "How to Create a Marketing Order," at www.ams.usda.gov /rules-regulations/moa/howto.

72. "Marketing Orders, Agreements Perform Different Functions."

73. See Administrative Committee for Pistachios (www.acpistachios .org/); and U.S. Department of Agriculture (www.ams.usda.gov/rules-regu lations/moa/983-pistachios).

74. Linda Calvin, "Outbreak Linked to Spinach Forces Reassessment of Food Safety Practices," *Amber Waves* (USDA, Economic Research Service, June 2007); Humphrey, "Food Safety, Private Standards Schemes and Trade," 33.

75. Calvin, "Outbreak Linked to Spinach Forces Reassessment of Food Safety Practices"; Humphrey, "Food Safety, Private Standards Schemes and Trade," 33; Shermain D. Hardesty and Yoko Kusunose, "Growers' Compliance Costs for the Leafy Greens Marketing Agreement and Other Food Safety Programs," *U.S. Small Farm Program Research Brief* (University of California, 2009), 2.

76. Hardesty and Kusunose, "Growers' Compliance Costs for the Leafy Greens Marketing Agreement and Other Food Safety Programs," 2.

77. Leafy Greens Products Handler Marketing Agreement, "About Us" (www.lgma.ca.gov/about-us/committees/).

78. "The California Leafy Greens Marketing Agreement" (www .farmfoundation.org/news/articlefiles/1819-363-scott%20horsfal.pdf).

79. Hardesty and Kusunose, "Growers' Compliance Costs for the Leafy Greens Marketing Agreement and Other Food Safety Programs," 2.

80. Humphrey, "Food Safety, Private Standards Schemes and Trade," 35.

81. Anahan O'Connor, "New York Attorney General Targets Supplements at Major Retailers," *New York Times* (blog), February 3, 2015 (http:// well.blogs.nytimes.com/2015/02/03/new-york-attorney-general-targets -supplements-at-major-retailers/?emc=eta1). Sen. Orrin Hatch (R-Utah) has successfully led the effort to keep dietary supplements free of any serious government regulation of the sort to which drugs are subjected. The industry itself has fought efforts to ensure quality and effectiveness. The result of having neither private nor public oversight is that consumers of these products have little idea what they are ingesting.

82. See the webpage of the FDA for more information about the law at www.fda.gov/AboutFDA/WhatWeDo/History/FOrgsHistory/CFSAN /ucm083863.htm.

83. Erin Quinn and Chris Young, "Why the FDA Doesn't Really Know What's in Your Food," Center for Public Integrity, April 14, 2015 (www .publicintegrity.org/2015/04/14/17112/why-fda-doesnt-really-know-whats -your-food).

84. See Stephanie Strom, "Many G.M.O.-Free Labels, Little Clarity over Rules," *New York Times*, January 30, 2015.

CHAPTER 6

1. Some trade specialists are also labeled "professionals," for example, plumbers, carpenters, electricians, beauticians, real estate agents, and bartenders. In most states those specialties require a license issued by the state after passing a skill-oriented exam. However, the professions of practice included in this study of nongovernment policymaking in almost all cases require at least one advanced academic degree beyond the four-year baccalaureate. See Arthur P. Coladarci, "What About That Word Profession?," *American Journal of Nursing* 63, no. 10 (October 1963): 116–18.

2. Eliot Freidson, "The Changing Nature of Professional Control," *Annual Review of Sociology* 10, no. 1 (1984): 1–20.

3. John W. Wade, "Public Responsibilities of the Learned Professions," *Louisiana Law Review* 21, no. 1 (December 1960): 130–39.

4. See the website of the Joint Commission for more information at www.jointcommission.org/.

5. See the website of the NCEES at http://ncees.org/.

6. Eliot Freidson, *Professionalism: The Third Logic* (University of Chicago Press, 2001), 105. For other sociological perspectives on professions, see Magali Sarfatti Larson, *The Rise of Professionalism: A Sociological Analysis* (University of California Press, 1977); Andrew Delano Abbott, *The System of Professions: An Essay on the Division of Expert Labor* (University of Chicago Press, 1988).

7. Carolyn J. Tuohy addresses the question of how to understand "the nature of the institutions which govern the acquisition and the application of specialized knowledge." See her "Private Government, Property, and Professionalism," *Canadian Journal of Political Science* 9, no. 4 (December 1976): 668–81.

8. This intrusion into the autonomy and best judgment of professionals is not limited to government. In the case of medicine in particular, private

insurers and health maintenance organizations can override physicians' diagnoses and treatment plans.

9. Note that the terms *higher education, colleges, universities, post-secondary institutions, schools,* and *colleges and universities* are used interchangeably here.

10. See U.S. Department of Veterans Affairs, "Education and Training," at www.benefits.va.gov/gibill/history.asp.

11. See National Center for Education Statistics, "Fast Facts," at http://nces.ed.gov/fastfacts/display.asp?id=98.

12. For a detailed breakdown of all funds appropriated by Congress to higher education, by category, see American Council on Education, "A Brief Guide to the Federal Budget and Appropriations Process," at www.acenet.edu/news-room/Pages/A-Brief-Guide-to-the-Federal-Budget-and-Appropriations-Process.aspx. For a news report on total student loan debt and one view of its impact, see Chris Denhart, "How the $1.2 Trillion College Debt Crisis Is Crippling Students, Parents and the Economy," *Forbes* (August 7, 2013), at www.forbes.com/sites/specialfeatures/2013/08/07/how-the-college-debt-is-crippling-students-parents-and-the-economy/.

13. National Science Foundation, "Find Funding" (www.nsf.gov/funding/).

14. As state appropriations dwindle, relative to the costs of higher education, public universities are making up for the shortfall with tuition hikes, contributions from graduates, and in other ways. The distinction between public and private education is less sharp than in the past; however, most public institutions were originally established by the states. In a few cases states have assumed responsibility for formerly private schools.

15. For an example of infringement on free speech rights by rescinding an offer to hire, see Colleen Flaherty, "AAUP Slams U of Illinois Handling of Steven Salaita Case," *Inside Higher Education* (April 28, 2015), at www.insidehighered.com/news/2015/04/28/aaup-slams-u-illinois-handling-steven-salaita-case.

16. More information about CHEA, including its stated purpose and principles, can be found on its website at http://chea.org/pdf/chea-at-a-glance_2012.pdf. CHEA publishes the renewal application materials of accrediting organizations it oversees and allows a time period for public comment.

17. Questions concerning the extent of government involvement in higher education policy are being raised by governments elsewhere. Two studies by one of the leading associations of universities in Europe explore this issue. See Thomas Estermann and Terhi Nokkala, *University Auton-*

omy in Europe I: Exploratory Study (2009) and Sybille Reichert, *Institutional Diversity in European Higher Education: Tensions and Challenges for Policy Makers and Institutional Leaders* (2009), both published by the European University Association (EUA), Brussels, Belgium.

18. Not all colleges accept government funding, a fact to which the existence of the exceptional Hillsdale College in Michigan attests. Since 1984, to preserve its autonomy from federal mandates, Hillsdale College has not allowed its students to bring federal funds to the college. See Hillsdale College website at www.hillsdale.edu/about/history for details.

19. This situation may be changing as new forms of credentialing are being developed in the wake of online education. It is also true that the more elite the college, the less needed accreditation actually is. One might argue that accreditors want Ivy League schools to participate in accreditation more than those schools need accreditation.

20. NACIQI was established under Section 114 of the Higher Education Act of 1965, as amended (HEA), 20 U.S.C. 1011c. Technically, NACIQI is an advisory body, as described in the *Federal Register:*

The NACIQI advises the Secretary of Education about:

The establishment and enforcement of the criteria for recognition of accrediting agencies or associations . . .

The recognition of specific accrediting agencies or associations or a specific State public postsecondary vocational education or nurse education approval agency.

The preparation and publication of the list of nationally recognized accrediting agencies and associations.

The eligibility and certification process for institutions of higher education under Title IV, of the HEA, together with recommendations for improvement in such process.

The relationship between (1) accreditation of institutions of higher education and the certification and eligibility of such institutions, and (2) State licensing responsibilities with respect to such institutions.

Any other advisory function relating to accreditation and institutional eligibility that the Secretary may prescribe.

(Federal Register, "National Advisory Committee on Institutional Quality and Integrity," www.federalregister.gov/articles/2015/06/15 /2015-14511/national-advisory-committee-on-institutional-quality -and-integrity-naciqi)

21. The term "buffer body" is used frequently in Europe where most universities are agencies of government. Buffer bodies were created to give universities some independence from government. Their membership includes university officials, faculty, and members of the general public. In most cases, government allocates funds to these organizations, which then decide how those funds should be allocated to universities. See, for example, Roger Brown, *Quality Assurance in Higher Education: The UK Experience since 1992* (London and New York: Psychology Press, 2004), xi and 26.

22. See Jamil Salmi, "Is Big Brother Watching You? The Role of the State in Regulating and Controlling Quality Assurance," Council for Higher Education Accreditation, Washington, D.C., 2015. For several years, Salmi was coordinator of higher education matters for the World Bank.

23. Uninterested in research activities, for-profits have been especially desirous of eligibility for federal student aid. For-profit institutions rely on tuition for over 90 percent of their revenues, while private four-year nonprofit institutions rely on tuition for 32 percent, according to the National Center for Education Statistics. Much tuition is financed by the taxpayers through grants and loans. Again the contrast between for-profits and nonprofits is notable. The percentage of students at four-year institutions receiving student loan aid was highest at private for-profit institutions (79 percent). In comparison, 62 percent of students at private nonprofit institutions and 51 percent of students at public institutions received direct student loan aid. See National Center for Education Statistics, "Postsecondary Revenues by Source," at http://nces.ed.gov/programs/coe/indicator _cud.asp.

24. Both accreditors are recognized by the U.S. Department of Education and the Council on Higher Education Accreditation.

25. For a well-argued critical view of for-profits in higher education, see Maura Dundon, "Students or Consumers? For-Profit Colleges and the Practical and Theoretical Role of Consumer Protection," *Harvard Law and Policy Review* 9 (2015): 375–401. Also see Kevin Kinser, *From Main Street*

to Wall Street: For-Profit Higher Education: ASHE Higher Education Report (New York: Wiley, 2006).

26. This reluctance by the regionals may have been justified. In 2015 the ACICS was apparently being investigated by the Consumer Financial Protection Bureau (CFPB) in its effort to "determine whether any entity or person has engaged or is engaging in unlawful acts and practices in connection with accrediting for-profit colleges," according to *Inside Higher Ed* quoting the CFPB. See Paul Fain, "Federal Watchdog Eyes Accreditor," *Inside Higher Ed*, October 15, 2015 (www.insidehighered.com/news/2015/10/15/federal-watchdog-seeks-information-national-accreditor-about-profit-colleges).

27. In 2012 the Senate Committee on Health, Education, Labor and Pensions, however, delivered a scathing report on for-profit colleges and their accreditors. According to the *Chronicle of Higher Education,* the committee concluded, "For-profit colleges can play an important role in educating nontraditional students, but the colleges often operate as aggressive recruiting machines focused on generating shareholder profits at the expense of a quality education for their students." Michael Stratford, "Senate Report Paints a Damning Portrait of For-Profit Higher Education," July 30, 2012, at http://chronicle.com.mutex.gmu.edu/article/A-Damning-Portrait-of/133253/.

28. Some of these include the Art Institute of Pittsburgh, Capella University, Kaplan University, University of Phoenix, DeVry University, Strayer University, and Walden University.

29. Though self-interested, the opposition was not entirely unfounded, as for-profits tended not to have tenured or research faculty, thus creating uneven cost comparisons between the two types of institutions and downplaying the importance of academic research and values. Now for-profits' having access to government funds through student grants and loans has apparently created a huge financial problem for the students who matriculated there and for the government. According to a recent study, in 2011 half of the loan recipients were students graduating from for-profit and two-year institutions (so-called nontraditional borrowers), but they comprised 70 percent of borrowers in default, many of whom never graduated. Of the top twenty-five colleges whose students owe the most, a majority (thirteen) are for-profit colleges. (Total student loan indebtedness is $1.2 trillion.) "What type of institution students attend matters: default rates

have remained low for borrowers at most 4-year public and private non-profit institutions, despite the severe recession and relatively high loan balances." See the report on Adam Looney and Constantine Yannelis, "A Crisis in Student Loans? How Changes in the Characteristics of Borrowers and in the Institutions They Attended Contributed to Rising Loan Defaults," *Brookings Papers on Economic Activity* (Fall 2015), at www.brookings.edu/about/projects/bpea/papers/2015/looney-yannelis-student-loan-defaults?hs_u=rudder@gmu.edu&utm_campaign=Brookings+Brief&utm_source=hs_email&utm_medium=email&utm_content=21977440&_hsenc=p2ANqtz-_kSfgf_ozKFX-Luz7wOa9fswFHtrRmsUKhtlDt0bjAB4eQdWOEKorabw8tX72Rq7baLsuwarBqPSTpXRP2X2bVeC77uw&_hsmi=21977440.

30. The European University Association, an informal group of university evaluators who use an evaluation process similar to the U.S. model, starts by telling an institution that the purpose of the evaluation is to "hold a mirror" up to the institution to see if, in the judgment of its own faculty and staff, it is doing well in fulfilling its mission statement.

31. The other four accrediting organizations are: the Accrediting Commission for Community and Junior Colleges; the New England Association of Schools and Colleges; the Southern Association of Colleges and Schools; and the WASC Senior College and University Commission.

32. For details, see the website of the New England Association of Schools and Colleges at www.neasc.org/.

33. For a full list (with links to the articles) on the CCSF situation from the *San Francisco Chronicle*, go to www.sfgate.com/ccsf/.

34. Daniel de Vise, "Southeastern University Loses Accreditation; Fall Term Unlikely," *Washington Post*, September 15, 2009, at www.washingtonpost.com/wp-dyn/content/article/2009/09/14/AR2009091401088.html. Also see Kevin Carey, "Asleep at the Seal: Just How Bad Does a College Have to Get to Lose Its Accreditation?" *Washington Monthly*, March/April 2010, at www.washingtonmonthly.com/features/2010/1003.carey.html.

35. Of course, Southeastern was located in Washington, D.C., which does not enjoy full representation in Congress.

36. For details on the American Medical Association, see www.ama-assn.org/ama. On the number of practicing physicians who belong to the AMA, see Roger Collier, "American Medical Association Membership Woes Continue," *Canadian Medical Association Journal* 183, no. 11 (August

9, 2011), at www.cmaj.ca/content/183/11/E713. First published July 11, 2011, doi: 10.1503/cmaj.109-3943.

37. For detailed information about the Liaison Committee on Medical Education, see its website at www.lcme.org/.

38. AMA Constitution at www.ama-assn.org.

39. See the AMA website at www.ama-assn.org/ama/pub/about-ama /our-mission.page?

40. Peter Whoriskey, "AMA Panel Takes Steps toward More Transparency," *Washington Post*, November 6, 2013; Peter Whoriskey and Dan Keating, "How a Secretive Panel Uses Data That Distorts Doctors' Pay," *Washington Post,* July 20, 2013.

41. Donna Marbury, "RUC Committee Takes Steps toward Transparency," *Medical Economics*, November 11, 2013, at http://medicaleconomics .modernmedicine.com/medical-economics/content/tags/aafp/ruc -committee-takes-steps-toward-transparency.

42. Ibid.

43. The Office of Professions of the Department of Education explains that "The Board of Regents, on the recommendation of the Commissioner of Education, appoints a State Board for each licensed profession to advise and assist the Board of Regents and the State Education Department on matters of professional regulation" (www.op.nysed.gov/boards/). Also see www.op.nysed.gov/ and www.op.nysed.gov/boards/.

44. The office's website states, "The mission of the Office of Professional Medical Conduct (OPMC) is to protect the public by investigating professional discipline issues involving physicians, physician assistants, and specialist assistants. OPMC is responsible for investigating all complaints of misconduct, coordinating disciplinary hearings that may result from an investigation, monitoring physicians whose licenses have been restored after temporary license surrender, and monitoring physicians, physician assistants, and specialist assistants placed on probation as a result of disciplinary action." See www.opnysed.gov/opd.

45. Office of Professional Medical Conduct, Board for Professional Medical Conduct: 1997 Annual Report (Department of Health, New York State, 1997) (www.health.ny.gov/professionals/doctors/conduct/annual _reports/1997/).

46. New York State, Department of Health, Medical Conduct Annual Reports. See www.health.ny.gov/professionals/doctors/conduct/annual_reports/.

47. In the somewhat boastful fact sheet, the Centers for Medicare and Medicaid Services (CMS) explains the new provisions that are aimed to reduce costs in "Better Care, Smarter Spending, Healthier People: Improving Our Health Care Delivery System" (updated January 26, 2015) at www .cms.gov/Newsroom/MediaReleaseDatabase/Fact-sheets/2015-Fact-sheets -items/2015-01-26.html. The act's formal title is the Patient Protection and Affordable Care Act (Public Law 111-148).

48. Centers for Medicare and Medicaid Services website at www.cms .gov/openpayments/index.html. The investigative journalism website Pro-Publica has created an ongoing series on physicians' financial conflicts of interests. See "Dollars for Docs: How Industry Money Reaches Physicians" at www.propublica.org/series/dollars-for-docs/.

49. *North Carolina State Board of Dental Examiners* v. *Federal Trade Commission*, U.S. No. 13–534 (decided February 25, 2015).

50. The law that the Bell Commission recommended was known as the Libby Zion Law, after the young woman who died. Barron H. Lerner, "A Case That Shook Medicine," *Washington Post*, November 28, 2006.

CHAPTER 7

1. Mary Williams Walsh, of the *New York Times*, is one member of the press who educates readers knowledgably about an aspect of private governance, the Financial Accounting Foundation's Financial Accounting Standards Board (FASB) and Governmental Accounting Standards Board (GASB).

2. To finally adopt such a rule, President Obama has turned not to the SEC, which had been dragging its heels since 2010 in moving to adopt this requirement, but to the Department of Labor. (The SEC could have regulated on its own or could have requested FINRA to act. It did neither.) Andrew Ackerman, "U.S. Tightens Broker Standards for Retirement Advice: Rules Would Require Recommendations That Are in Investors' Best Interest," *Wall Street Journal,* April 14, 2015. As Ackerman explains, "Under the proposal . . . brokers would have to put clients' interests ahead of personal gain when they make recommendations for retirement accounts. At present, brokers' recommendations only have to be 'suitable,' a weaker standard that critics have said permits products with high fees that slowly erode returns."

3. Giandomenico Majone, *Evidence, Argument, and Persuasion in the Policy Process* (Yale University Press, 1989).

4. Mónica Brito Vieira and David Runciman, *Representation* (Cambridge, U.K.: Polity, 2008). For more on the Extractive Industries Transparency Council, see Virginia Haufler, "Disclosure as Governance: The Extractive Industries Transparency Initiative and Resource Management in the Developing World," *Global Environmental Politics* 10, no. 3 (2010): 53–73.

INDEX

Accountability: after-the-fact, 47, 48, 49, 89; approaches to, 47; before-the-fact, 48–49; of collective food standards, 110–11; as contextual, 49; definition of, 46–47; of higher education accreditation, 140–41; minimum standards of, 58–59; principal-agent concept and, 47–48; of private governance, 4–5, 6, 12, 37; procedure and, 51; representation and, 24, 49–51

Accounting firms, performance of, 63–66

Accreditation, 103. *See also* Higher education accreditation; Joint Commission on Accreditation of Health Care Organizations

Accrediting Commission for Community and Junior Colleges, 135

Accrediting Council for Independent Colleges and Schools (ACICS), 131–32

ACCSC (American Commission of Career Schools and Colleges), 131–32

Administrative Procedure Act, 51, 52

Affordable Care Act, 147–48

After-the-fact accountability, 47, 48, 49, 89

Agencies: delegation to, 29–30; hybrid, 11, 21; need for expertise by, 30–34, 41; rulemaking by, 1–2

Agricultural Marketing Agreement Act, 113